W9-CQB-387

Gardening with Flowers

A Wisley Gardening Companion

Gardening
with
Flowers

GRAHAM RICE AND

KAY N. SANECKI

Cassell

The Royal Horticultural Society

THE ROYAL HORTICULTURAL SOCIETY

Cassell Educational Limited
Villiers House, 41/47 Strand
London WC2N 5JE
for the Royal Horticultural Society

First published 1994

British Library Cataloguing in Publication Data
A catalogue record for this book is available from
the British Library

ISBN 0–304–34410–9

Photographs by Pat Brindley, Iris Hardwick Library
of Photographs, Roger Hyam, Andrew Lawson,
Photos Horticultural, Graham Rice, Paul Roberts,
Harry Smith Collection, Peter Stiles

Line drawings by Mike Shoebridge

Phototypesetting by RGM Associates, Southport,
and Litho Link Limited, Welshpool, Powys

Printed in Hong Kong by Wing King Tong Co. Ltd.

Page 1: *Papaver oriental* 'Black and White' has attractive
seedheads once the petals drop; it is best propagated from
root cuttings
Page 2: *Crocus ancyrensis* provides a cheerful start to the
year, but it needs sunshine to persuade the flowers to open

Contents

Foreword

It gives me great pleasure to introduce another of the Society's Wisley Gardening Companions. This volume, *Gardening with Flowers*, brings together three more in the popular and long-established Wisley Handbook series: *Herbaceous Perennials, Bedding Plants* and *Fragrant and Aromatic Plants*. Bound together they offer a wide selection of flowering plants and excellent advice on how to grow them well.

Most people, when they think of a garden, think of flowers – I know I do. Flowers not only provide colour and seasonal interest, but also in many cases fragrance. Some flowering plants go on year after year, marking the seasons with their display; hellebores and lungworts in spring give way to the more flamboyant Oriental poppies, peonies and day lilies of summer, while Michaelmas daisies and sedums herald autumn. This is the reliable cycle of herbaceous perennials, but many gardeners require something more. Plants for impact, flowers for tubs and hanging baskets – and it is here that bedding plants prove their worth. Old favourites like lobelia, tagetes and zonal pelargoniums have established their place in this market. But added to these are the tender perennials – trailing verbenas, ferny foliaged lotus and multi-coloured lantana are just a few of the exciting plants that have become more widely available in recent years.

To complete the flower garden and of primary importance to many, is fragrance. You may immediately think of roses, lilac and lavender, but what more delightful experience could there be than encountering on a bleak winter's day the delicate perfume of winter-sweet or *Viburnum farreri*?

> Gordon Rae
> Director General
> The Royal Horticultural Society

Argyranthemum 'Jamaica Primrose', *Salvia farinacea* 'Victoria' and *Helichrysum petiolare* 'Limelight'

Herbaceous Perennials

GRAHAM RICE

Hemerocallis, eremurus, *Campanula lactiflora*, plume-like macleaya and lavatera bring colour to a mixed border in summer

Introduction

WHAT IS A HERBACEOUS PERENNIAL?

This is a question that often provokes lively discussion among gardeners. The definition given in *The New RHS Dictionary of* *Gardening* is 'perennial plant which dies down to the ground annually', but this only provokes more questions: Surely this definition also includes bulbs? What about pinks and all the other 'herbaceous perennials' which are evergreen? Does it include bergenias, which are not only evergreen but also have stout woody stems? And how about fuchsias, undeniably shrubs yet prone to behave as herbaceous perennials in many gardens?

Argument will doubtless continue, but we have to draw the line somewhere. And of course the solution must be both practical and pragmatic. So our line corresponds with that customarily drawn by gardeners – perhaps tentative but nevertheless clear.

It is not evading the issue to say that this section covers those plants which most people refer to as herbaceous perennials, and which feature in books and catalogues under that heading. This, of course, includes delphiniums, phlox and Michaelmas daisies, whose stems and leaves die down completely every year. Hellebores are in, despite the fact that some have stems or leaves which persist over the winter; so, too, are euphorbias. I do not include bulbs, which clearly come in a well-defined category of their own. Neither do I admit fuchsias, phygelius, caryopteris or perovskias which, although they may be cut down to the ground by frost or secateurs, are undoubtedly shrubs. Bergenias are clearly not shrubs, so they also find a place here. Also included are a few plants which are sometimes classified as alpines for although some epimediums and gentians are widely grown by alpine enthusiasts, I have included those which are suited to more general planting.

This being but an introduction to the subject, the range of plants I can cover is limited. Of course, I have included all the major perennials which are found in garden centres, specialist nurseries and seed catalogues. But experience, personal preference, and personal opinion have influenced my selection of cultivars.

Part of the splendid herbaceous borders at Arley Hall, near Northwich, Cheshire

Where to Grow Perennials

There are two strands to the developing use of herbaceous plants in gardens. In herbaceous borders and island beds, perennials have exclusive right to the territory and indeed these features have been developed specifically to show off perennials to their best advantage. Yet herbaceous perennials have also been grown in cottage gardens where they have taken their chance with the fruit, the herbs and the chickens. And in mixed borders with a wide variety of other plants, the perennials often contribute to the success of the whole.

HERBACEOUS BORDERS

In large gardens herbaceous plants are traditionally grown in the herbaceous border, a formal planting usually backed by a wall or yew hedge. The plants are arranged in groups which are kept separate and not allowed to intermingle. Generally, the tallest are planted towards the back, grading to the shortest at the front. A border of this sort makes an impressive feature, especially as at Arley Hall and Newby Hall, where parallel borders are separated by a grass path. It is at its best in the summer months.

The annual maintenance of such a border consists of lifting, dividing and replanting perhaps one-third each year, digging and enriching the soil with organic matter at the same time. Plants are set out in groups of three, five or more depending on the size of the border. Between replantings, the border is given a dressing of general fertiliser each spring, and it may also be mulched. The hoe is used between the plants until their foliage meets and smothers any weeds. Staking is one of the most important jobs in such a border but it is time-consuming and can be an expensive business. The whole border is usually cut down in the autumn and the sections not due for replanting forked over lightly and left tidy.

At its peak such a border can be stunning, and immediately

Island beds at Bressingham Gardens where the taller plants are grouped towards the centres of the irregularly-shaped beds

before and afterwards it can still look pretty good. In a garden large enough to accommodate other plants for other seasons the herbaceous border will undoubtedly appeal as an impressive way to feature perennials. In winter, however, it will be undeniably bleak, and planting too many spring and autumn flowering plants will detract from its impact in summer. Moreover, certain aspects of its maintenance are time-consuming, in particular the regular replanting and, as mentioned, staking.

ISLAND BEDS

The island bed is a concept developed by Alan Bloom of Bressingham Gardens as a way of displaying perennials without the necessity of a formal border set against a hedge or wall. Informal beds, often laid out in sweeping curves, are designed to be viewed from all sides. The size and shape of the beds are arranged according to the space available. They may be roughly oval or kidney-shaped but are not normally rectangular in outline.

The beds are planted with the taller varieties towards the centre. The plants grown are those which are self-supporting, generally those of naturally short growth, or shorter-growing varieties of naturally tall plants. The advantages of growing perennials in island beds are that such plantings can be fitted into gardens and situations not suitable for a traditional herbaceous border and that the use of dwarfer cultivars virtually eliminates the time-consuming task of staking.

COTTAGE GARDENS

In cottage gardens and in modern cottage-style plantings hardy perennials take their chance in the rough and tumble with all the other plants. Traditionally, plants which are easy to divide have long been cottage favourites, and this explains why in many villages you tend to see the same plant in almost every garden. The same goes for plants which self-sow easily. Either way, the perennials have had to hold their own with the shrubs, fruit, vegetables, herbs and sometimes poultry. Those that require pampering have tended to fade away, while the more invasive among them had chunks heaved from them and discarded. This accounts for the unlikely plants sometimes found in hedgerows near villages. So, with occasional human intervention, the cottage garden has settled into an uneasy equilibrium, with shade-loving plants finding homes either under the shrubs and fruit or under taller perennials.

THE MIXED BORDER

It could be argued that a mixed border is little more than a sophisticated version of a cottage garden. Small trees, evergreen and deciduous shrubs, climbers, hardy perennials, bulbs, some of the tougher alpines, annuals, biennials and bedding plants, plus ground-cover plants of all descriptions, are grown together in a carefully planned and thoughtfully maintained planting. It is in the mixed border that the art of associating plants is brought to perfection, so that the whole is more effective than the sum of its parts.

Hardy perennials play a crucial role in this increasingly popular approach to planting and will often be the most numerous plants. Popular because the mixed border can not only be adapted to any situation in a garden of any size but also because the use of so many other kinds of plants enables us to realise our aims more effectively. In particular, whereas an island bed or herbaceous border can be bare and featureless in winter, it would be hard to achieve the same result in a genuinely mixed border.

There are other ways of growing hardy perennials. A bed may sometimes be set aside for just one favourite – though it had better be a good one – or for a single group of plants like delphiniums or peonies. A few selected cultivars can be grown very effectively in meadows, while some are ideal for containers, either as single specimens or in mixed plantings.

A cottage garden where herbaceous perennials mingle with roses and annuals – all in delightful profusion

Colour Schemes and Plant Associations

Growing healthy plants should be the aim of all gardeners but if the plants are arranged badly, the garden will still be a disappointment. Learning to group plants together so that they enhance one another can take time and requires a discriminating eye. Looking at other well-planted gardens and taking note helps immeasurably. The easiest way to create a colourful display is to choose plants which enjoy the same conditions and flower at the same time, and then to plant them all in a single border. Colourful, yes, but satisfying?

There are a number of factors which you need to consider when planning your planting: height, growth habit, time of flowering, flower shape and colour, foliage shape, texture and colour, and secondary attractions such as seed heads.

HEIGHT

It almost goes without saying that you should not put very short plants at the back of the border where you cannot see them. Yet there are exceptions. In a herbaceous border which is planned to be at its best in June, snowdrops, primroses and anemones can be planted all the way through, even at the back, for when they flower there will be almost no growth in front to obscure them. Furthermore, the old idea of growing all the tall plants at the back and all the short ones at the front does give a rather formal, regimented look to the border. By planting some of the taller ones in groups which reach forward in the border you can create a more interesting effect.

HABIT

Plants vary in the way they grow. A border full of plants that develop into rounded hummocks would look strange. On the other

The evergreen Gladwyn iris, *Iris foetidissima*, displays spectacular fruits when the seed pods split open (see p. 60)

19

hand, consciously planting a mixture so that no two plants of the same habit are next to each other will have no spark. Look at the growth habits of the individual plants and treat each case on its own merits.

FLOWERING TIME

Many people like to make gardens which 'look attractive all the year round' and this is perfectly reasonable and possible. But it is exceptionally difficult to achieve this in just one bed or border. For if you plan a relatively small space for year-round interest, at each season there are one or two plants at their peak, yet the border itself never looks stunning – there are always plants which are a long way before or after looking their best. Planning borders to be at their best for a restricted season at least ensures they will be colourful. And even in relatively small gardens, planning several beds or even corners to be at their best at different seasons is a very effective way of organising your planting. This ensures that there is always one area which is at its best while another fades and another is ready to follow on.

FLOWER SHAPE

Flowers come in a huge range of shapes and sizes and are carried in a wide variety of different ways. Daisy shapes, trumpets, spikes – whatever. You can have fun with these in two ways. Contrasting a plant with stiff spikes of flowers such as *Salvia × superba* with another like *Achillea* 'Gold Plate', which flowers in flat heads, is very effective (see opposite). Likewise, choosing plants of similar habit but with different individual flowers and in varying colours also works very well and is eye-catching, as, for example, yellow kniphofias and blue veronicas.

FLOWER COLOUR

This is the one aspect of plant association which attracts everyone – and of course it is important. But it is also a trap for the unwary. Many gardeners see the single colour border as a way of taking the angst out of planning. But creating attractive borders around narrow colour themes is much more difficult than it sounds. White is a popular colour theme but only when the border blooms may the realisation dawn that there are many variations of white – and that they do not always go together. One particular irritation can be that unopened buds or fading flowers may take on yellow, blue, green or pink tints. Blue borders are also popular but, again, there are so many different blues! And the purplish ones do not always fit with the sharper shades.

A slightly looser approach can often be successful, one that imposes guidelines but does not restrict you to a single colour. Blue, pink and silver borders work well; so, too, do fiery borders in bronze, red, orange and yellow. Combining a couple of harmonious colours, perhaps with a sympathetic foliage shade, gives the whole border a more relaxed feel, although without abandoning a theme.

FOLIAGE SHAPE AND TEXTURE

A blend of contrasting foliage shape and texture can be very satisfying, especially as foliage lasts for so much longer than flowers. The variety is almost endless. There is the broad, bold foliage of plants like hostas, sword-like irises and lacy ferns. Bergenias are glossy, stachys is woolly, bugles metallic and meconopsis rough.

A splendid contrast in colour and form is achieved through the association of *Salvia × superba* with *Achillea* 'Gold Plate' (see pp. 65 and 47)

Combinations that involve thoughtful use of these qualities repay close inspection.

FOLIAGE COLOUR

Leaves, too, vary in colour. Most, of course, are green but if this gives the impression that they are all the same, this is far from true. The more you look at leaves the more the word 'green' is revealed as encompassing colours that deserve quite different names. In addition to all those greens, leaves come in various yellow-tinted shades through to deep gold; in blues through to grey; and in coppers, bronze, purples and reds. Variegated leaves may cover combinations of all these even if the pale-edged or pale-splashed forms are the most common.

This multiplicity of variation can be treated in a number of ways. Some gardeners use it as a theme in itself and plant single-colour, even yellow- or grey-leaved, borders, sometimes realising only too late that these plants also carry flowers. I find the best approach is

Above: Hostas are invaluable foliage plants, with leaves in many shades of green. Some, like 'Frances Williams', are beautifully variegated (see p. 59)
Opposite: The flower heads of bergenia grow up through the shiny evergreen foliage to bring welcome colour to the garden early in the year

to treat foliage as simply another colour to be worked into the mix. Lasting longer, it provides continuity but needs as careful association with other plants as do flowers.

SECONDARY ATTRACTIONS

Many plants have secondary features which come into their own before or after their prime season, and these can augment or detract from the border on either side of the central display. Autumn colour, fruits and seed heads, tinted early foliage – these are important features which can bring colour to a bed or border out of its main season. The colours and forms at this time of year must either be planned as thoughtfully as for the main season or you must be prepared to take a chance and risk a few surprises. Just to give some hints of possible ways to go about things, here are some examples of effective associations involving hardy perennials. I would urge you, nevertheless, not to follow them slavishly, but to come up with your own ideas and develop your own tastes.

Summer foliage in shade A blue hosta like 'Halcyon', lacy ferns such as *Athyrium filix-femina* with *Iris foetidissima*.

Winter foliage in shade Bold, richly coloured *Bergenia* 'Bressingham Ruby' and the silvery white *Lamium maculatum* 'White Nancy' in front, with the white-striped *Iris foetidissima* 'Variegata' behind.

Winter flowers in shade Smaller dark-leaved bergenias like 'Abendglut' for background, *Pulmonaria rubra*, winter aconites and snowdrops.

Spring flowers in shade Purple hellebores, white wood anemones and pale blue *Pulmonaria* 'Fruhlingshimmel'.

Spring flowers in sun Limy yellow *Euphorbia characias*, the brighter *Cheiranthus* 'Bredon', apple green *Helleborus argutifolius*, rich purple *Pulsatilla vulgaris* and honesty.

Summer flowers Pink and white *Lavatera* 'Barnsley', blue spikes of *Campanula persicifolia*, *Anaphalis margaritacea* for grey foliage with white flowers to follow, and the long-flowering pink *Geranium endressii* 'Wargrave'.

Blue and yellow flowers Arching shoots of *Mertensia pulmonarioides*, pale lemon *Narcissus* 'Hawera', sparkling blue *Omphalodes cappadocica* 'Cherry Ingram' with yellow-eyed blue violets like

Vigorous *Crocosmia* 'Lucifer' opens its fiery red flowers from mid-summer

'Ardross Gem' and perhaps the yellow flowers and red foliage of *Euphorbia amygdaloides* 'Rubra' for contrast.

Fiery flowers *Crocosmia* 'Lucifer' with *Dahlia* 'Bishop of Llandaff' plus orange and rusty heleniums.

Horizontal and vertical Flat heads of *Achillea filipendulina* 'Gold Plate', upright spikes of deep blue *Salvia* 'May Night' with dainty, foamy *Coreopsis* 'Moonbeam' in front.

Cultivation

SOILS

There are no soils in which it is impossible to grow perennials; indeed there are plenty of good examples suitable for most soils. The oft-quoted ideal of a rich, well-drained, medium loam is one which few of us can aspire to but we should not be downcast. Moist soils can be improved sufficiently to allow a very wide choice.

Soils which cannot be drained and so remain waterlogged for much of the year may still be planted effectively by choosing the right plants. Dry soils, too, benefit from careful plant choice but are easily improved to suit a wider range.

The enthusaist for perennials is far luckier than the shrub fanatic when it comes to lime. Many of the most sought-after shrubs such as rhododendrons and pieris hate lime and thus are beyond the reach of many gardeners. Perennials are less fussy and although some, like lupins, may prefer an acid soil, failing this they will still thrive.

SITUATION

There is a wide choice of plants available for most situations. This is not so much because hardy perennials are adaptable (though many are) but rather that perennials grow naturally in such diverse habitats and so many kinds are available, that there are always plenty suited to any particular spot. So in sun or shade, wind or sea spray, on slopes or level ground, indeed anywhere you suggest, there are perennials to fit. But since not all are adaptable, it remains important to choose the right plant for the right place. Do not simply put a plant you like into a space you happen to have available.

Furthermore, there are ways of making seemingly inhospitable areas more acceptable to plants. You might build a raised bed to give a greater depth of soil; thin or remove the lower branches of a

A mixed border with the silver foliage of Stachys lanata and the giant thistle-like Onopordon, combined with frothy lime-green Alchemilla mollis

tree to let in more light; or plant evergreens for shelter. Just a little forethought can widen the range of possible plants enormously.

PREPARATION

Thorough preparation of beds and borders is the single most important thing you can do to ensure that your plants thrive. If you wish to grow perennials in mixed borders, then double digging will be valuable – though as much for the shrubs as the perennials. For island beds and herbaceous borders thorough single digging will suffice.

Always consider the drainage. Laying drains is a major job, and if you are surrounded by other gardens where is the run-off to go? A soakaway only has a limited capacity. Sometimes compaction is the cause of poor drainage, and this can be remedied by double digging. Add plenty of organic matter at the same time. I feel that forking it into both the lower spit and the upper spit is preferable to leaving it in layers. In most situations thorough single digging will be quite sufficient.

Organic matter such as well-rotted farmyard manure is excellent, though not always easy to come by. Good garden compost is a close second, and there are various other materials like spent mushroom compost (it *must* be sterilised), composted bark and the many soil conditioners which have come on the market since we have become aware of the need to avoid using peat on the garden. It will bear restating: do *not* use peat as a soil conditioner.

The other important job is to remove weeds. They can be removed by hand as you go through. It is imperative to remove all perennial weed roots as any that are left will only cause trouble later – when it is so much more difficult to deal with them.

If the area is obviously weedy, it will pay to deal with the weeds first, before cultivation begins. Spraying with glyphosate will kill most; I find that a second application a fortnight after the first gives the best results. If you prefer, it is just as effective to cover the whole area in opaque black polythene or old carpet to smother weed growth, although this takes much longer to work.

PLANTING

After all the work on the soil, there are final preparations to be done before actually planting. The bed or border should be knocked down roughly level with the fork and then raked to give an even finish. It must then be trodden to ensure there are no air spaces;

otherwise sinkage will be uneven. A little extra levelling may be needed at this stage. A dressing of fertiliser is advisable before planting. Raking in a handful of a general fertiliser such as blood, fish and bone or Growmore to each square yard will give the plants a flying start. If you are planting in the autumn, leave the fertiliser application until the spring as the winter rain will only leach it away before the roots get a chance to use it.

In the days after preparation assemble as many of the plants as you have to hand. Planting can take place whenever the soil is not frozen, sodden or parched. But only in spring or autumn will you be able to plant both pot-grown and bare-root plants together with any to be moved from other parts of the garden. Generally I would suggest September, October, late March or April as the best planting times. My personal instinct is to plant in spring, as growth will start almost at once, whereas in autumn there is no way to protect plants against winter's frost and rain.

Some autumn-flowering plants such as chrysanthemums and Michaelmas daisies are best left until spring unless planted from pots; and even if the rest of the bed is planted in the autumn, it is wise to leave a few others until the winter is over. These include lobelias and penstemons, which are not reliably winter hardy in all areas, and some which object to winter wet like catananche, pyrethrums, anthemis, scabious and gaillardia. Simply mark their sites and leave them in the frame until April.

Choose a day without extremes for planting; cool, still and humid conditions suit both plants and planter. You may have a plan drawn out, but in any event you should have given some thought to the planting scheme before confronting the empty bed at your feet. Set the plants out on the bed where they are to go, preferably marking positions for bare-root plants initially with canes to avoid exposing the roots to the elements. Almost without exception, perennials look better planted in groups of three, five, six, seven or eight than as single plants. This does not necessarily mean buying three of everything, as many newly bought perennials can be knocked out of their containers and immediately split.

Plant small plants with a trowel, large ones with spade. The best general rule is to set them just a fraction lower in the soil than they were previously growing and to firm them well. Plants dug from the open ground, either in the nursery or from your own garden, should have their roots spread out well unless they have a good root ball, in which case this should be retained as far as possible. Work from a board on heavy soil to avoid compaction. Be sure to firm the plants in well, but use fingers in preference to boot, especially on heavy soil. Autumn-set plants will need checking during the winter as frost and heavy rain can leave them loose in the soil or expose the roots. Ensure the plants are well labelled.

After planting, water each plant thoroughly. It is also a good idea to add a liquid feed to help give them a flying start. The simplest way to water a large planting is with a sprinkler, but try to avoid wasting water. I usually start by watering in from a can. It is vital to prevent container-grown plants from drying out in the summer after planting.

When planting and watering are completed the soil should be lightly pricked over to leave it looking neat. Finally, if weed-free organic matter is available in liberal quantities, the whole bed can be mulched.

The story is similar when planting a group of perennials or adding a single plant to an existing planting. The site should be forked over and organic matter mixed in, followed, as before, by treading and application of fertiliser. Beware of hidden bulbs and self-sown seedlings which may be disturbed.

MULCHING

Regular mulching makes an invaluable contribution to the success of hardy perennial plantings. A good mulch helps retain moisture, thus removing the need for quite so much irrigation, keeps down weeds, feeds the plants and in the long run improves the soil.

Mulch should be well rotted, friable and weed free. Only the best garden compost meets all three criteria – the third being the most often wanting. Farmyard or stable manure is probably the best choice but it may need stacking to allow it to finish rotting. Spent mushroom compost is excellent, though limy, but it must be sterilised to to kill mushroom fly larvae. Peat is now not an option as a mulch but the many soil-conditioning peat substitutes are ideal. Never use lawn mowings as they invariably contain weed seeds, especially annual meadow grass.

The time to mulch depends to some extent on the type of planting. In a herbaceous border or island bed, early spring is ideal, but in mixed and cottage plantings, where there may be very early plants like snowdrops and aconites, autumn is preferable.

FEEDING

If you prepare well and are able to use a rich mulch on a regular basis, feeding may be totally unnecessary. If you use no mulch at all, feeding is essential. For many gardeners, supply and demand governs the frequency of mulching any given bed, so mulching one year and feeding the next is a reasonable compromise. A handful of blood, fish and bone or Growmore to the square yard in early spring, raked in lightly, is all the plants need. These are general fertilisers that many gardeners possess and which can be bought economically in large sacks. I find that various specific feeds are unnecessary, although sometimes individual plants benefit from an occasional liquid feed.

WATERING

In recent years a succession of drier summers have led to widespread restrictions on the use of sprinklers. The best way to reduce the need for watering is to add plenty of organic matter during preparation, to mulch well and regularly, and to choose plants carefully for the different situations in your garden.

When it comes to using the sprinkler (standing with hosepipe in hand, or tying it to the handle of a fork are equally useless methods) a thorough watering every couple of weeks is far more effective than a skimpy one every couple of days. Choose a sprinkler to suit your beds. Long, straight formal borders are best watered with a square pattern, oscillating sprinkler, while for beds in sweeping curves a pulse sprinkler which waters circles and segments of circles is less wasteful. Do not forget that you need a licence from your local water company for a sprinkler.

WEEDING

Weeds need particular attention in the preparation and early years of herbaceous plantings, but once established, even the most upright of hardy perennials should produce a sufficiently dense cover to smother the majority. Assuming the roots of perennial weeds are removed during preparation, mulching will deal with most weeds as long as the mulch itself is weed free. In the absence of mulching, hoeing is effective early in the season, even in mature borders, although self-sown seedlings are likely to be decapitated along with the weeds. There are two rules to all weeding which apply here as anywhere else: never let any weeds set seed and always remove perennial weeds the moment you spot them.

Occasionally bindweed, ground elder or other particularly tenacious weeds appear in the clumps of perennials and can quickly take a hold. The simplest trick is to paint the leaves with a weedkiller aproved for use in this way. Bindweed can be untwisted first. However, if perennial weeds appear under a newly set plant, it is better to dig up the plant, remove the weed roots and then put the plant back.

STAKING

In island beds, the majority of the plants grown are usually short, stocky and self supporting. But tall and weak-stemmed plants, those in open positions and in traditional borders often need support and this must be done as unobtrusively as possible. Brushwood (pea sticks) is the traditional supporting material. Hazel is by far the best as it comes in convenient flat, fan-shaped sprays. Birch is sometimes more readily available but you need bigger quantities and it is more obtrusive. Neither is easy to come by, although local nature conservation groups who may be managing woodlands are often a good source.

Surround the plants with the brushwood and loop string around the outside and across the middle to secure it well. The top 12 in (30 cm) can be broken over to a horizontal position for the shoots to grow through. Alternatively, set bamboo canes 12–18 in (30–45 cm) apart around the edge of a group, wind string round them and cross it over between the canes. For tall single-stemmed plants like delphiniums, single canes are sometimes used, each stem being tied in individually with two or three loose ties of soft string. Wire supports in a number of styles are now available and are convenient, unobtrusive and very effective. They can be expensive to buy but should last for many years. Whichever system you choose, the supports must be the right height and must be in place early in the season. Judging the height can be tricky as growth can vary from year to year. Most plants need support to about half or two-thirds of their eventual height, or to just below their leafy growth. In gardens with large borders, it is useful to record the correct staking heights in a notebook for future reference.

Stakes should always be in position early in the season so that plants are supported as they grow rather than propped up after collapsing. This can mean that for a few weeks canes or brushwood are more obtrusive than you would like, but the shoots weave through them as they grow and they will be well hidden later.

The soft ferny foliage of delphiniums soon covers the stakes necessary to keep these tall plants upright

REPLANTING

Many perennials need regular lifting and replanting to keep them in good health and flowering well. They can be lifted in autumn or spring, choosing the strongest and healthiest pieces from the outside of the clump for replanting (see Propagation, page 38). Various plants need this treatment for different reasons. Shasta daisies (*Leucanthemum × superbum*), heucheras and bergenias tend to grow out of the ground, exposing woody growth. Michaelmas daisies (*Aster*) produce the best flowers from strong young shoots. Monardas, crocosmias, some campanulas, achilleas, some asters and others simply creep too far and need restraining.

Conversely, there are some plants that are best left undisturbed to make impressive clumps. These include hostas, hellebores, rheums and peonies.

DEADHEADING

The flowering period of many plants can be extended by regular removal of dead flowering shoots just above the first set of leaves below them. Salvias, phlox and anthemis will usually bloom for longer, while delphiniums and Shasta daisies will look much neater. Some plants will flower again later in the year if the flowering stems are cut out entirely. Many more will grow fresh, attractive new foliage if cut down right to the ground when flowering is over. Plants which benefit in this way include astrantias, achilleas, doronicums, Oriental poppies (*Papaver*) and many cranesbills (*Geranium*). Apart from improving their appearance, all plants benefit from deadheading as it diverts their energy from seed production to fattening up the roots. It also prevents prolific seeders such as achilleas from producing vast numbers of unwanted seedlings.

There is one situation, of course, where dead heads should not be removed. If the seed heads themselves are attractive they are best left on the plant right through until spring. Grasses, sedums and astilbes fall into this category.

END OF SEASON

At some point in the dormant season borders need tidying: some people like to do it in the autumn, others in the spring. Autumn is the traditional time. When the last Michaelmas daisies and other asters are over, you can usually get to work – unless there are naturalised colchicums or autumn flowering crocus in the border! First remove the stakes and supports, then cut out dead stems at ground level and get rid of all the debris; the woodiest material is ideal for the base of the compost heap. Next, remove weeds and gather up fallen leaves, which can also go on the compost heap. Any replanting or dividing can now be done and labels checked and rewritten. Fork the whole border over lightly to neaten it up and expose soil pests to your friendly robin. Finally, apply a mulch.

There are two problems with this autumn treatment. Late autumn-flowering plants are becoming increasingly popular and thus may still be in flower in November. Also, dead stems can look very attractive in winter, especially when coated with frost. So you may prefer to leave the whole job until the spring.

Geranium renardii is one of the more unusual cranesbills, ideal for the front of a sunny border (see p. 55)

CULTIVATION CALENDAR

Spring
○ Do not tread on heavy soil after rain.
○ Apply a general fertiliser such as blood, fish and bone or Growmore.
○ Plant newly received plants; heel them in for planting later if conditions are bad.
○ Stake any plants that need support; see to early flowering subjects like peonies first.
○ Tie delphiniums and other spire plants to canes as they grow.
○ Lift and divide plants that resent the process in autumn or which were overlooked.
○ Hoe between clumps if the border was not mulched in autumn.
○ Check that perennial weeds are not emerging in the centre of clumps.
○ Beware of emerging bulbs when working amongst the plants.
○ Deadhead early-flowering plants like doronicums as necessary.
○ Water newly planted borders or groups if necessary.
○ Fill gaps with appropriate summer bedding plants and hardy or half-hardy annuals.
○ Prevent slug damage to hostas and other susceptible plants using pellets or other treatments.
○ Look out for aphids, capsids, thrips, caterpillars and other pests and treat accordingly.
○ Order new plants for autumn and spring planting.

Summer
○ Check that plants are not evading their supports.
○ Lift and divide flag irises after flowering.
○ Deadhead as flowers fade; pay special attention to columbines (*Aquilegia*), achilleas and other prolific seeders.
○ Cut back Oriental poppies (*Papaver*), astrantias and similar plants to encourage a flush of fresh foliage.
○ Water newly planted borders or single groups if necessary. Be prepared to spot-water flagging plants.
○ Watch for weeds which have evaded the hoe, mulch or steely eye.
○ Continue to look out for pests, mildew and grey mould.
○ Order new plants for autumn and spring planting.

Autumn
○ Continue to deadhead to prevent carpets of self-sown seedlings.
○ Plant new borders and groups, lift and divide most perennials.
○ Start digging and preparing new beds as soon as possible.

Winter
○ Cut down dead stems and clear away to the compost heap. Do it early or late as you choose.
○ Keep off the border when the soil is wet.
○ Order new plants for spring planting.

Mixed asters include *Aster* × *frikartii* and Michaelmas daisies (see pp. 48 and 49), seen here with a yellow kniphofia

Propagation

One of the great attractions of hardy herbaceous perennials is that most are so easy to propagate. Many can be raised from seed; most can simply be lifted, divided and replanted, whereupon they will grow away well. Some propagate themselves all too easily.

DIVISION

Almost all hardy perennials can be divided, although some resent it and some increase so slowly that division is only possible after several years and yields few young plants.

The process is easiest with plants like Michaelmas daisies (*Aster*) with their loose, fibrous roots system, while peonies and hellebores are more difficult. In almost all cases there will be some old, tired and woody growth which is best discarded. The youngest growth, usually at the edge of the clump, is the best for propagation.

Most plants can be lifted and divided in the autumn. First dig up the clump and shake off a little of the soil. A few plants such as flag irises can simply be pulled and broken to yield pieces suitable for replanting. Plants with open, fibrous growth can be split using the famous two forks method.

If you find it difficult to see exactly where to divide tightly congested clumps of plants like hellebores or polyanthus, wash the soil off, using a hosepipe, and cut the plant into individual crowns with a knife or secateurs.

Plants with exceptionally tough, dense growth such as hostas can be treated differently. They should be divided *in situ* with a knife to avoid disturbing the roots any more than necessary. Plant the small divisions either directly into the border in improved soil or line them out for a season to make bigger plants before moving them to their flowering positions.

Finally, do not be afraid to divide newly bought plants. Many in 4–5 in (10–13 cm) pots, and sometimes those in smaller ones, can be divided into two, three or four pieces straight away. This applies especially to plants like achilleas, schizostylis and crocosmias which produce short runners.

The two forks method. Push the two forks vertically through the middle of the clump, back to back; then break the clump in two by working the handles together and pulling them apart. The process can be repeated to break up the clump further, at which point it is usually possible to pull off strong shoots for replanting.

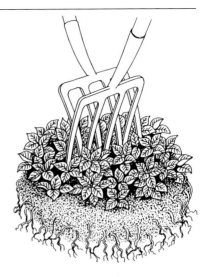

Using a spade. Alternatively, use a spade to cut vertically through the middle of the clump. This can even be done with the plant still in the ground so that one half at least is disturbed relatively little. It sounds brutal but large clumps possess enough crowns to be able to spare one or two being sliced off.

Propagating from thongy roots
1. Lift the plant, wash off some of the soil and cut off a few roots roughly the thickness of a pencil and about 2–3 in (5–7.5 cm) long. Cut the top square and the bottom slanted so that you can tell the top from the bottom.

2. Fill a 5 in (13 cm) pot with the same compost as used for cuttings, leaving a 1 in (2.5 cm) gap at the top. Insert the cuttings vertically in dibber holes so that the top of each cutting is level with the compost.

3. Top with ½ in (12 mm) of grit and water in well. Then leave the pot in a cold frame for the roots to develop shoots. In spring they can be potted up individually and planted out when large enough.

Using a knife. If you do not wish to disturb a specimen clump, use an old bread knife to cut and remove a triangular segment like a slice from a cake. Then fill the resulting hole with fresh soil.

CUTTINGS

Many hardy perennials can easily be increased from stem cuttings if taken at the right time – spring for most species. As a rule, shoots should be 3–4 in. (7.5–10 cm) long and not hollow. Sever them close to the crown, even with a heel, using a very sharp pair of secateurs. Timing varies with the plant and season, so watch from February onwards those you wish to increase. This method only works with plants with recognisable stems, such as delphiniums and anthemis, not with those whose flowers and leaves spring from the base.

Bag and label the cuttings as you go then trim cleanly, removing lower and damaged leaves. Use pots or trays with 50 per cent proprietary cuttings compost and 50 per cent perlite or grit – most composts stay too wet unless grit is added. Bury the cuttings deep enough to hold them upright, but no deeper, and place in an unheated propagator in the greenhouse or on a windowsill. Shield from strong sun to avoid scorching and check for botrytis (grey mould). When rooted, pot up individually, harden off if necessary and grow them on outside or in a frame until ready for planting.

Propagating from fibrous roots
1. If you only want a few plants, there is no need to lift the whole plant, simply scrape away the soil from the roots and cut off sections of fibrous root 3–4 in (7.5–10 cm) long.

2. Lay these out flat on the surface of compost in seed trays and cover with about ¼ in (6 mm) of compost.

3. If you require more plants, lift the whole plant and prepare as many roots as you need. Then gather them into bundles of about ten, tie with raffia or soft twine, and insert vertically as if they were one fat root cutting. When they begin to shoot, separate them for potting individually.

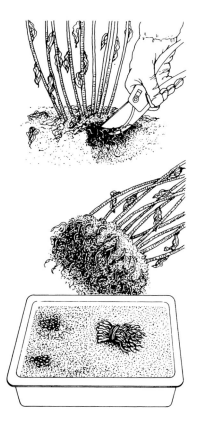

ROOT CUTTINGS

Some plants will root from winter root cuttings. There are two groups: those with fat, thongy roots, such as Oriental poppies (*Papaver*), anchusa, globe thistles (*Echinops*) and *Crambe cordifolia*, and those with fine, fibrous roots such as phlox, which require a slightly different method (see illustration opposite).

SEED

This is the ideal method for many plants. However, some cultivars will not produce identical seedlings so must be increased by division or cuttings. Particularly recommended for raising from seed are alchemillas, alliums, columbines (*Aquilega*), delphiniums, foxgloves (*Digitalis*), hellebores, sweet peas (*Lathyrus*), lupins, meconopsis and pulsatilla.

Most perennials can be sown in spring and are not all that fussy. Use good quality John Innes Seed Compost or soil-less seed compost in pots or trays. Sow in March or April and place in a propagator, warm or frost-free greenhouse, cold greenhouse, cold frame or even outside in a sheltered spot. After germination, prick out into trays or individual pots and as the seedlings mature plant into beds and borders or line them out first to grow on for a while. Early sowing and lining out is especially valuable for seed which is sold in mixtures, as the plants will often produce a small flower spike late in their first summer, enabling you to check colours.

Sowing in the open ground in summer works well for many plants, especially if you have plenty of seed. Others need a period of cold before will they germinate. Sowing hellebores in July can give almost 100 per cent germination, usually before Christmas, but from seed kept until January very few are likely to germinate. Pulsatillas, many primulas and gentians are also best sown fresh and left in a cold frame or north-facing spot outside, where they will get frost in winter. This is needed to encourage germination, usually occurring in the spring.

Pests and Diseases

Compared with indoor plants, hardy perennials are not troubled by many pests and diseases, although some of those which are troublesome can be especially debilitating. If your plants are grown well, they are generally less likely to be attacked, and less likely to be killed if they are. Growing plants in a soil and situation which suits them, giving them the individual care they need, feeding, watering and mulching will give them strength to ride out any attack which may occur. Fortunately, hardy perennials are tough plants, so perhaps we should show a little tolerance. There is no need to rush for the sprayer at the first sign of an aphid or to fill it with the most lethal potion on the garden centre shelf. Pinching off diseased shoots, physically squashing caterpillars and similar basic methods can be very successful if attended to regularly.

PESTS

Aphids
The most common pest, aphids come in a wide range of sizes and colours and debilitate plants by sucking sap; they also transmit virus diseases. The fat grey ones which attack lupins are especially prolific.
Organic control: Squash with fingers, or use insecticidal soaps.
Chemical control: Spray with pirimicarb which spares most beneficial insects.

Capsids
Insects up to $\frac{1}{4}$ in. (6 mm) long suck sap from the shoot tips and the leaves develop small irregular holes as they expand. Most common in late spring and summer.
Organic control: Pinch out shoot tips, clear away debris and garden waste.
Chemical control: Spray with malathion, pirimiphos-methyl or dimethoate, concentrating on shoot tips.

Euphorbia characias subsp. *wulfenii* 'Lambrook Gold' is one of the most stately and impressive herbaceous perennials (see p. 55)

Earwigs

The familiar earwigs chew petals, especially of double and fleshy flowers like chrysanthemums, dahlias, delphiniums and Michaelmas daisies; they also sometimes eat flower buds and young leaves.
Organic control: Clear rubbish, trap insects under old sacking or cardboard, up-end flower pots stuffed with straw on canes as traps.
Chemical control: Spray at dusk with malathion or pirimiphos-methyl when damage is seen.

Leather jackets

These daddy-long-legs larvae are especially common when new beds are made in lawns. Grey-brown larvae up to 2 in. (5 cm) long feed on roots and young shoots, especially in spring.
Organic control: Fork over new beds a couple of times to allow birds to get at the larvae.
Chemical control: Generally impractical although slug pellets containing methiocarb may have some effect.

Slugs and snails

Probably the most destructive of all pests, especially in damp springs, they eat young shoots of a wide variety of plants as well as tubers and bulbs.
Organic control: Clear away debris which provides daytime hiding places. Use slug killers based on aluminium sulphate. Hand pick by torchlight on mild damp evenings.
Chemical control: Use slug pellets containing methiocarb or metaldehyde. Do not leave in large heaps; single pellets at 4 in. (10 cm) intervals are just as effective.

Wireworms

Orange-brown larvae about 1 in. (2.5 cm) long tunnel into stems, roots, bulbs and tubers, particularly in spring. Most common on newly cultivated ground.
Organic control: Cultivate ground well before planting to allow birds to feed. Keep weeds under control.
Chemical control: There are no direct chemical controls.

DISEASES

Stem and leaf rots

A variety of different rots attack stems, leaves and flowers of many different plants including chrysanthemums, delphiniums, carnations (*Dianthus*) and peonies. The result is rotting crowns, grey mould on foliage and flowers, brown rots on stems and leaves.

Organic control: Difficult, but improving drainage can sometimes help. Spray with colloidal sulphur.
Chemical control: Spray with benomyl, carbendazium or thiophanate-methyl and repeat according to the manufacturer's instructions. Dust crowns with a proprietary fungicide.

Leaf spots

A number of plants including peonies, hellebores, aquilegias, campanulas and irises can suffer from various leaf-spotting problems, especially in wet conditions.
Organic control: Difficult: colloidal sulphur will deal with some.
Chemical control: Diseases on different plants respond to different fungicides; benomyl, a copper fungicide and mancozeb are among the most effective.

Powdery Mildew

A white powdery coating spreads over stems and foliage, leaves eventually go yellow and drop off. In dry conditions and in crowded borders this disease can attack a wide variety of plants. Although the appearance is generally similar, each plant often has its own specific mildew which will not spread to different plants.
Organic control: Spray with colloidal sulphur.
Chemical control: Spray with benomyl, carbendazim, fenarinol or thiophanate-methyl.

Root and foot rots

Many apparently unexplained deaths of a wide range of plants are the result of these rots which are caused by a variety of fungi. Wilting or feeble growth may be the first sign of trouble.
Organic control: Thriving plants are much less susceptible, so growing plants well is half the battle. Dig up and burn infected plants and replace with a plant of a different type. Improve cultivation, especially soil quality, drainage and pH levels.
Chemical control: There are no direct chemical controls.

Virus

Virus diseases are becoming increasingly common especially on hostas, lilies, primroses, wallflowers (*Cheiranthus*), chrysanthemums and delphiniums. Symptoms vary but include poor growth, distorted foliage, pale streaking or mottled leaves, poor flowering, difficulty in propagation and streaky and distorted flowers.
Organic control: Dig up and burn affected plants. Control the aphids which often spread the viruses.
Chemical control: None.

—— Recommended Perennials ——

Choosing from the vast range of hardy perennials available to gardeners is a thankless task. There will always be individual favourites which are not included or given but scant attention. When in doubt, however, I have given preference to those whose popularity is increasing. This is, after all, intended as an introductory book; there are comprehensive volumes for gardeners who crave information on more plants and in more detail.

Acanthus Sumptuous foliage plants with large, glossy leaves making impressive but often invasive clumps 4–5 ft (1.2–1.5 m) high. *A. mollis* 'Latifolius' has floppy, broadly divided leaves. In *A. spinosus* the leaves are broader, deeper green and tipped with spines, while the slightly silvered 'Spinosissimus' is more finely cut and even more spiny. All are happy in sun or shade but flower best in the sun, their spikes of pink or purple two-lipped flowers rising through the foliage in late summer.

Achillea Easy but often invasive plants, good for unimproved soils. All have flat heads of flowers over attractive, finely cut foliage and thrive in most soils in at least half a day's sun. *A. millefolium* and its various hybrids, 2–3 ft (60–90 cm), can be invasive but are excellent in new gardens. Many fade horribly but exceptions include 'Forncett Fletton' (opposite) in orangey brick red, 'Hoffnung' in sandy yellow and the dark purplish red 'Burgundy'. 'Moonshine' is a more clumpy hybrid with grey foliage and pale yellow flowers. *A. filipendulina* 'Gold Plate' (see p. 21), is taller and more stately at 4 ft (1.2 m) with broad, bright yellow heads which look wonderful behind upright salvias. The white buttons of *A. ptarmica* 'The Pearl', 2–3 ft (60–90 cm), are pretty but the plant runs and seeds rather too freely.

Aconitum Summer- and autumn-flowering plants with good foliage and spikes of hooded flowers, usually in blue. 'Bressingham Spire', 3 ft (90 cm), is purplish blue, 'Blue Sceptre', 2 ft (60 cm), has blue and white bicolored flowers; both are self supporting. 'Newry Blue', 5 ft (1.5 m), is much more stately but needs support. Rather different are the creamy flowered 'Ivorine' and the yellowish *A. vulparia* which will scramble through shrubs or fall through an

---

The warm orangey tones of *Achillea* 'Forncett Fletton' associate well with mauve flowers, such as heliotrope or Michaelmas daisies

earlier flowering perennial. Good soil and full sun or partial shade suits them well. The tuberous roots are poisonous.

Alchemilla Almost every garden now features the limy yellow flowers and slightly downy leaves of the delightful A. *mollis* – but it does self-sow freely. Wonderful in front of blue irises or with diascias, but you should be ruthless with the seedlings or they will crowd out other plants. Thrives in most reasonable soils and situations.

Anemone The Japanese anemones are invaluable late-flowering plants and though difficult to move and often slow to establish, once settled they spread well, sometimes too well. All those listed under A. *hupehensis*, A. *japonica* and A. × *hybrida* are very similar with their running roots, deeply toothed foliage and elegant stems carrying single or semi-double flowers in various pinks or white. The plant usually listed simply as A. × *hybrida*, 5 ft (1.5 m), is shimmering pink. 'Honorine Jobert' is similar but purest white. 'Bressingham Glow' is half as tall and a semi-double warm pink. All appreciate full sun, a heavy soil and space to run.

Anthemis Easy and reliable daisies in two groups, both growing well in sun and any reasonably well-drained soil. The various forms of A. *tinctoria*, 3 ft (90 cm), flower exuberantly for many weeks in summer. 'Grallach Gold' is rich yellow, 'E. C. Buxton' paler and sharper; both need staking with brushwood. They are often short-lived, but cutting back hard when the flowers fade is a help, as is regular replanting with the strongest divisions. Lower and more spreading is the invaluable A. *cupaniana*, 12 in. (30 cm), with fine, silvery foliage and white daisies from spring to autumn.

Aquilegia Columbines come in a great variety, the only constant factor being their promiscuous tendency to hybridise. New seed or plants from a reliable source are the only ways to ensure correctly named stock. There are many hybrid selections from the compact Music, 15 in. (38 cm), to the McKana Hybrids, 3 ft (90 cm), while the fully double pink, white and green 'Nora Barlow' is an old favourite. All these thrive in any rich but well-drained soil in sun or partial shade but they are not long-lived. For species like the red and yellow A. *canadensis*, 2–3 ft (60–80 cm), and the deep olive green A. *viridiflora*, 15 in. (38 cm), good drainage is even more necessary.

Aster The Michaelmas daisies are a mixed lot – some fine plants but others tall and floppy; many suffer from mildew. Some of the New England asters, A. *novae-angliae*, 4 ft (1.2 m), are disease and pest resistant and more or less self-supporting; try the warm-toned 'Harrington's Pink', the positively lurid pink 'Andenken an Alma Potschke' and the pure white 'Herbstschnee' ('Autumn Snow') (see p. 50). The true Michaelmas daisy, A. *novi-belgii*, is more variable and includes dwarfs like the 10 in. (25 cm) 'Lady in Blue', but some are prone to mildew. These make up only one group; among the many other invaluable asters are the lavender-blue *A. × frikartii* 'Mönch', 18 in. (45 cm) (see p. 37), which flowers all summer and autumn, and *A. lateriflorus* 'Horizontalis', 2 ft (60 cm), with clouds of tiny lilac and pink flowers. All are tolerant plants thriving in any reasonable soil and a sunny situation; they are best divided every three or four years.

Astilbe Tough, densely spreading plants with good foliage and self-supporting spires of foamy flowers. They come in reds, pinks and white and range in height from 12 in. (30 cm) to 4 ft (1.2 m). Astilbes revel in wet or water-retentive soil and full sun but will also do well in slightly drier spots if given a little shade. 'Sprite', 12 in. (30 cm), is pearly pink with metallic foliage, 'Fanal', 18 in. (45 cm), is deep red while 'Deutschland', 2 ft (60 cm), is white and 'Amethyst', 3 ft (90 cm), is lilac-pink.

Astrantia Easy to grow, self-supporting, and self-seeding plants with intriguing pincushion flowers surrounded by a ruff of bracts. They are also blessed with good weed-suppressing foliage and are happy in any reasonable soil in sun or dappled shade. The naming is a little confused but among those to look out for are *A. major* with greenish white flowers and *A. maxima* with a pink-tinted cushion and pink bracts. 'Shaggy', also known as 'Margery Fish', has especially well-developed bracts. 'Hadspen Blood' is deep red. 'Sunningdale Variegated' (see p. 50) has yellow- and cream-margined foliage. All reach about 2 ft (60 cm).

Bergenia Sometimes known as elephant's ears, from the broad, rounded foliage, these tough evergreen perennials are splendid for early colour though the flowers are sometimes frosted. Their foliage is valuable all the year round. For good foliage choose 'Bressingham Ruby', the crimson-flowered 'Abendglut' and *B. cordifolia* 'Purpurea' with their rich winter colour. Others to look for are the dwarf pink 'Baby Doll', the big and bold crimson-flowered 'Ballawley' and the stunning pure white 'Beethoven'. Bergenias are sometimes relegated to the driest of shade where they survive but do not thrive. Good soil and sun produces the best leaves and impressive early spring flowering.

Campanula A huge group covering tall plants for the back of the border to neat edgers. They come mainly in blue or white, although there are a few pinks and reds. *Campanula lactiflora*, 5–6 ft (1.5–1.8 m), is one of the tallest with straight stems breaking into bushy heads of flowers. 'Prichard's Variety' is purplish blue and there is also a white form. The lovely blue *C. persicifolia*, 3 ft

49

(90 cm), is more manageable, its slender stems lined with elegant open bells. There is a white form as well as doubles, semi-doubles and cup-and-saucer types in both blue and white. The cup-and-saucer 'Hampstead White' is charming. Coming down in scale again is a group with a creeping habit and tubular flowers, speckled inside. *C. punctata*, 12–18 in. (30–45 cm), has pink-tinted flowers with darker spots inside, *C. takesimana*, 2 ft (60 cm), is lilac-tinted with maroon spots. For the very front, *C. carpatica*, 9–12 in. (23–30 cm), has cup-shaped flowers over mounds of neat foliage. There are many cultivars, from the deep blue 'Karl Foerster' to 'White Clips'. Most like sun or partial shade and any reasonable soil that is not too waterlogged – in fact the conditions to be found in most gardens. They can be prone to slug damage and it pays to deadhead promptly to encourage a second flush.

Chrysanthemum Now mostly correctly called *Dendranthema*, the garden chrysanthemums are among the most valuable of late-flowering plants. Those in the Rubellum group, 2 ft (60 cm), are especially free-flowering and reliable and include 'Clara Curtis' in a clear pink and 'Duchess of Edinburgh' in coppery red. The hardy hybrids vary from the 4 ft (1.2 m) 'Emperor of China' with silvery pink flowers in November to the 2 ft (60 cm) 'Mei-Kyo' with neat dark pink buttons. There are plenty more, almost all good. Two other fine species, both with single white daisies, are the neat, very late-flowered, 12 in. (30 cm) *C. yezoense* (now *Dendranthema yezoense*) and at the other extreme the 6 ft (1.8 m) *C. uliginosum* (now *Leucanthemella serotina*). Earlier than all these are the Shasta daisies (now *Leucanthemum × superbum*), with large, white, anemone-centred or double flowers. They are stiff and upright and need something bushy in front to cover their stems. 'Starburst' is a large single, 'Snowcap' is only 12 in. (30 cm) tall, 'Phyllis Smith' has rather a frilly look with narrow petals, 'Cobham Gold' is creamy centred, 'Esther Read' is short and fully double. Most reach about 3 ft (90 cm). All are at their best in full sun or when shaded from the east and in a good soil. Few will need staking unless grown in too shady a spot.

Above left: New England asters, such as *Aster novae-angliae* 'Herbstschnee', are reliable and welcome for their late-flowering habit (see p. 48)
Above right: Feathery astilbes multiply quickly, and even the taller cultivars do not require staking. They flower throughout the summer
Below left: A clump of *Astrantia* 'Sunningdale Variegated' brings brightness to a garden border with its attractive foliage (see p. 49)
Below right: The herbaceous clematis *C. integrifolia* has silvery seedheads which continue the period of interest after the petals fall (see p. 52)

Clematis The best known of these unsung heroes are *C. heraclei-folia*, 3 ft (90 cm), and *C. integrifolia*, 2 ft (60 cm) (see p. 50), but there are many other good but almost unknown species. The former makes a spreading plant with clusters of blue flowers in the upper leaf joints: 'Wyevale' is the one to look for. *C. integrifolia* is rather floppier, needs a shrub for support, and has the apparently un-promising trait of carrying just one flower at the tip of each shoot. Fortunately, some of the cultivars like 'Olgae' have branched flower heads. These are good border plants for sun and any reason-able soil, tolerant and strong, but generally in need of thoughtful support.

Crocosmia Vigorous spreaders, most of which are better than the montbretia so often seen in cottage gardens. 'Lucifer', 4 ft (1.2 m) (see p. 25), has arching shoots lined with tubular fiery red flowers and boasts pleated sword-shaped foliage; 'Star of the East', 3 ft (90 cm), has outward-facing apricot yellow flowers on upright shoots; 'Solfaterre', 18 in. (45 cm), has smoky bronze foliage and yellow flowers. There are many more. Although most are tough and tend to spread well, all prefer a soil that is not too limy and are at their best in a slightly moist climate. Some are tender in colder areas.

Delphinium These are among the most popular and impressive of the taller border perennials, but are often seen in poor forms raised from second-rate seed stocks. Grow cultivars obtained from specialists or the best seed selections. The best seed-raised selections are the New Century Hybrids, Blackmore & Langdon Strain and Southern Noblemen, 5 ft (1.5 m), all originating in Britain; the American Pacific Giants are less hardy and rather vari-able. Even with these selections it pays to grow the young plants in rows for a year and then pick the best, in preferred colours, for moving to the border. The plants raised from single colour seed selections will vary slightly in shade. All need full sun, a good fertile soil, protection against slugs in the spring and secure staking to avoid calamities. Cut them down after flowering and be pre-pared to spray against mildew.

Dianthus Garden pinks, 12 in. (30 cm), come in such a profusion of cultivars that recommending the best is far from easy. They can conveniently be divided into the old-fashioned pinks, which are mostly scented but once-flowering, and the modern pinks, which tend to flower for longer but may have less scent. Most are double flowered and all have the added benefit of grey-blue foliage in varying degrees. Of the older ones I like the wonderfully scented 'Mrs Sinkins' in pure white, though the flowers are untidy; 'Sops in

Wine' in white with an almost black edging; and 'Brympton Red' in crimson marbled with an even deeper shade. Of the modern ones the dark-eyed, pale pink 'Doris' is well known and there are a number of other good cultivars with forenames. 'Devon Cream' is an unusual creamy shade with a hint of pink, and 'Huntsman' is deep red. All thrive in sunny, well-drained places and love lime. They are ideal edgers.

Diascia These long-flowering sprawlers, 10–12 in. (25–30 cm), are good in most soils in sunny places but the colour range is limited to various pink shades. Although vigorous, they die out if not divided and the best pieces replanted almost every year. They are not hardy in the coldest areas. 'Ruby Field' is more a deep pink than ruby, D. vigilis is a lovely pale pink while D. integerrima is probably the darkest.

Dicentra A mixed genus, including creeping woodlanders, early border plants and even climbers. Bleeding heart, D. spectabilis, 2 ft (60 cm), is a wonderful plant with pink or white flowers swinging from arching stems. The young growth is both early and rather soft so is easily damaged by frost; a west-facing border is ideal. Many of the woodland types have greyish foliage and are great colonisers. 'Stuart Boothman' has soft pink lockets hanging over grey, much divided foliage. In 'Snowflakes', the foliage is greener and less divided and the flowers are white; 'Bacchanal' is deep red. All make classy ground cover in partial or full shade if the soil is not dry.

Doronicum Among the most brilliant of early flowers with cheerful bright yellow daisies in April and May. D. caucasicum 'Magnificum' is a good seed-raised form, 'Miss Mason' is a reliable old cultivar with good foliage; both reach about 2 ft (60 cm). 'Spring Beauty' is a little shorter and double flowered. All thrive in sun or partial shade and any good soil. They are best moved in autumn.

Echinops Tall spiny plants with silvery stems and globular heads of blue flowers. Wonderful at the back of the border but they may need support. Best in full sun, they thrive in poor soil and are inclined to run. E. ritro, 4 ft (1.2 m), is steely blue, even in bud, with silver-backed green leaves. E. bannaticus 'Taplow Blue' is slightly taller and is altogether greyer in foliage and stem with richer blue flowers.

Epimedium Increasingly popular creeping woodlanders, 10–15 in. (25–38 cm), with open sprays of intriguing spidery flowers and attractively tinted spring foliage. Many new kinds are now appearing. Most are deciduous but a few have evergreen foliage and these include E. perralderianum with glossy leaves and bright yellow flowers. Almost all the deciduous sorts are worth growing, but I would pick these: *E. grandiflorum* has a number of cultivars and both 'Rose Queen' and 'White Queen' are delightful; *E. davidii* has long-spurred, bright yellow flowers; and *E. × rubrum* (below) has especially well-tinted young foliage and deep pink flowers to match. All prefer a cool, dappled spot with leafy or peaty soil, but some, especially the evergreens, are surprisingly tolerant. Trim off the old foliage of both sorts just as the new shoots start to grow in early spring.

Eryngium The sea hollies provide some of our best blues and often combine their round or spherical heads with blue-tinted or white-veined foliage. The names, unfortunately, are rather muddled. The richest blue is found in *E. × oliverianum*, 2 ft (60 cm). *E. planum* is taller and has much smaller flowers but far more of them and in a similar deep shade. Our native sea holly, *E. maritimum*, 12 in. (30 cm), has broad grey leaves and pale blue flowers, while *E. bourgatii*, 2 ft (60 cm), has the best foliage, deeply cut and white-veined but with grey-green flowers. The eryngiums are an altogether tolerant group for almost any soil that is not waterlogged, although they do prefer full sun. Sea holly is best in very well-drained soil.

Euphorbia An increasingly popular group, the evergreens are almost shrubby and provide indispensable winter foliage and spring flowers. Many of the truly herbaceous ones are at their best rather later. There are now quite a few kinds of the evergreen *E. characias*, 2–4 ft (60 cm–1.2 m), available. All make upright stems

Epimedium × rubrum is a useful plant for a shady spot. Although grown primarily for its foliage, it has dainty pink flowers in spring

lined with narrow, sometimes blue-tinted foliage, topped with cylindrical heads of greeny yellow flowers, dark-eyed except in subspecies *wulfenii*. 'Lambrook Gold' (see p. 42) is especially impressive. All are good and grow in a variety of positions but are at their best in hot, dry sites where they will probably self-sow. Similar in habit is *E. rigida*, 18 in. (45 cm), with stunning silvery blue foliage and yellow flower heads, but this demands sun and good drainage. A little later comes the truly herbaceous *E. polychroma* with brilliant acid-yellow flowers, an easy and tolerant plant, though best in the sun. Later still is *E. sikkimensis*, 4 ft (1.2 m), which runs at the root. It starts the year with red shoots pushing through the soil, develops white-veined leaves along its stems and tops them with greenish yellow flowers in early summer. Unlike many, it prefers a damp soil and will stand partial shade.

Gentiana Most gentians are alpines but a couple are fine perennials. The willow gentian, *G. asclepiadea*, 3 ft (90 cm), needs woodland conditions and its arching branches are lined with pairs of sparkling blue flowers. You would hardly know *G. lutea* as a gentian; 4 ft (1.2 m) high, upright, with clusters of yellow flowers at the leaf joints, it needs rich but not wet soil and full sun.

Geranium The cranesbills are immensely popular and come in a huge, and still increasing, range of species, hybrids and cultivars. I can only include a small selection. *G. endressii* and its hybrids make low, dense, weed-suppressing cover and flower for many weeks. 'Wargrave Pink' is an especially bright colour, 'Claridge Druce' is vigorous with slighly greyish foliage. 'Russell Prichard' flowers from June to October and spreads widely from a central rootstock. For further back in the border the summer-flowering *G. pratense*, 2 ft (60 cm), comes with single and double flowers in various blues and white. 'Plenum Violaceum' is a neat double, 'Galactic' is fine pure white. Those who like black flowers always look out for *G. phaeum*, 2 ft (60 cm), with its dainty reflexed blooms, but it varies from deepest maroon to lilac and even white. My favourite is *G. renardii*, 12 in. (30 cm) (see p. 35). Not a typical cranesbill, its soft foliage has the texture and colour of sage leaves and sets off the white, purple-veined flowers beautifully. It makes a dense, rounded mound and needs a sunny spot at the front of the border where you can admire its markings. At its best a little earlier than most, *G. sylvaticum*, 3 ft (90 cm), is lovely in dappled shade. Naturally violet-blue in colour, 'Mayflower' is especially richly coloured with a white eye. Finally, *G. × magnificum*, 2 ft (60 cm), whose floppiness irritates some gardeners but whose rich, purplish blue, dark-veined flowers and long season win over so many more.

Geum The low, rough foliage may be undistinguished but the open sprays of flowers are delightful. Two seed-raised doubles, 2 ft (60 cm), the fiery red 'Mrs Bradshaw' and the yellow 'Lady Stratheden', are floriferous but their strong shades need careful placing. 'Borisii' is shorter and a warmer orange shade. All thrive in any reasonable soil in sun or partial shade.

Helenium These valuable summer- and autumn-flowering perennials are tough plants, producing a good show even in poor conditions. But they repay better soil, regular division and thoughtful support with sheets of flowers in yellow, rusty, coppery and chestnut shades. They range from the 2 ft (60 cm) orange-flowered 'Wyndley' to the 5 ft (1.5 m) orangey brown 'Moerheim Beauty'.

Helleborus Good hellebores are much sought after. Forget the cultivars propagated by division, which are almost impossible to find, expensive and not necessarily what they say they are. Modern selections are better and are offered more regularly. The *H. orientalis* hybrids, 18 in. (45 cm), are the most captivating but also the most variable. Surprisingly tolerant garden plants, they are at their best in rich, limy soil in dappled shade. Modern selections are your best choice and you can now choose from white, various pinks, reds and purples, slaty blues, pure greens and primrose yellows – all with or without spots. These selections also have much better

Above: Hellebores and pulmonaria, an effective combination of shade-tolerant perennials which flower in spring
Opposite: Yellow *Kniphofia* 'Little Maid' is a useful accent plant and softer in colour than the more familiar red hot pokers (see p. 60)

shaped flowers than most old cultivars. The Christmas rose, *H. niger*, 12 in. (30 cm), rarely flowers in December and is unhappy in some soils; but if your soil is well drained yet rich you should be able to grow it. The large-flowered 'Potter's Wheel' and the smaller but more floriferous 'White Magic' are impressive improvements on unselected seedlings. Two species with tall stems are easy to grow. *H. argutifolius*, 3 ft (90 cm), with apple green flowers and jagged foliage is best in the sun. The stinking hellebore, *H. foetidus*, 2 ft (60 cm), with small green cups edged in red, thrives in shade; 'Wester Flisk' is an impressive red-stemmed form. Hellebores are best left undivided for up to ten years to grow into imposing clumps, then divided in late summer.

Hemerocallis Day lilies compensate for opening each flower only for a day by producing them in a long succession. Modern hybrids have greatly extended the flowering period, reduced the height and improved the colour range. Many are scented. They are also tough, although they may need a favoured position and good drainage in the very coldest areas. 'Stella d'Oro', 18 in. (45 cm), is one of the newer, shorter cultivars with slightly peachy yellow flowers. The even newer 'Pardon Me' in deep red is equally dwarf, while 'Little Grapette', 12 in. (30 cm), is deep purple. Among the taller ones 'Corky', 3 ft (90 cm), is pale yellow, 'Mallard', 3 ft (90 cm), is rich red and 'Varsity', $2\frac{1}{2}$ ft (76 cm), is creamy peach with a maroon eye.

Heuchera Enjoying a revival with the introduction of new hybrids, heucheras, 2ft (60 cm), thrive in well-drained soil in full sun but often give a good display in shadier and damper conditions. Many have good foliage and the slender stems lined with flowers from May to July come in an increasing range of colours; they are good for cutting. 'Palace Purple' has rich purple-bronze foliage and cream flowers, 'Snowstorm' has white-splashed foliage and red flowers. 'Greenfinch' has green flowers while in a stronger colour there is 'Scintillation' in bright pink.

Hosta Ever popular and appearing in a continuing stream of new forms, hostas are superb ground-cover plants for sun or shade and remarkably tough. With their sumptuous foliage in a generous range of leaf colours and variegations – not forgetting their pale flowers – they are indispensable. The rich green *Hosta lancifolia* has fine narrow leaves overlapping like fish-scales; 'Royal Standard' is much more imposing. 'Thomas Hogg' and the slightly more stylish 'Shade Fanfare' have good white-edged foliage. *H. fortunei* 'Aureo-marginata' and the rather smaller 'Golden Tiara' are yellow edged. *H. fortunei* 'Aurea', the neater growing 'Golden Prayers' and the very large and slug resistant 'Sum and Substance'

Lobelia 'Queen Victoria' is a bold plant which prefers a moist well-drained situation (see p. 60)

are all-gold. Of the blues, *H. sieboldiana* 'Bressingham Blue' is tall with puckered foliage. 'Krossa Regal' is even larger, 'Halcyon' is the best of the smaller blues while the ever popular 'Frances Williams' (see p. 23) has yellow-edged blue leaves. For flowers, 'Honeybells', 'Royal Standard', 'Sugar and Cream', 'Sum and Substance' and *H. tardiflora* are among the best. Hostas are best left undisturbed to grow into fat clumps. In a rich soil and partial shade, they need only protection from slugs and snails and a regular mulch to keep them happy.

Iris Irises are essential border plants and although the flowers all have the same general appearance they come in many colours. Flag or bearded irises are the traditional cottage-garden iris. Those flowering in April and May are shorter than the many June-flowering cultivars. The dwarf types, 12–24 in. (30–60 cm), are ideal for small borders and gravel gardens. The June flags, 4 ft (1.2 m), are splendid border plants whose foliage is valuable after their relatively fleeting flowering season. Recommending cultivars is impossible – there are so many and they come in such an extraordinary range of shades, including maroons and yellows, that no one could be disappointed. They all like a sunny spot in almost any reasonably well-drained soil and are best divided and replaced every three or four years immediately after flowering. *Iris sibirica*, 3 ft (90 cm), is altogether different, with narrow upright foliage and a taste for damp soil. Its colours are restricted to blues, purples and white. The soft blue 'Papillon' is worth looking out for. These are best divided in early spring. For the hottest, driest spots *I. unguicularis*, 2ft (60 cm), is essential and is at its happiest at the foot of a south facing wall. Sometimes starting to flower as early as November and continuing to April, its scented flowers appear among grassy foliage but need protection from slugs. *I. foetidissima* 2 ft (60 cm) (see p. 18), is splendid for dry shade but thrives more heartily in better conditions. The deep green evergreen foliage is striking, its pretty flowers may be small but its sparkling orange-red berries are carried on arching shoots all winter. They usually self-sow.

Kniphofia Red hot pokers are no longer restricted to red and one of the most sought after is now 'Little Maid', 18 in. (45 cm) (see p. 57), in ivory cream with green buds. 'Bressingham Comet' is a deep orange and even shorter. If you like tall traditional types, go all the way with the fiery red 'Prince Igor', 6 ft (1.8 m). Kniphofias are happiest in well-drained soil in full sun and are best divided in spring rather than autumn. They may need protection from frost and winter wet in more northerly areas.

Lobelia Perennial lobelias have a reputation for lack of hardiness but slugs and rots seem more of a problem than frost. Their upright growth and richly coloured flowers, coupled in some cases with beetroot red foliage, make them invaluable for borders which are not too dry. 'Queen Victoria' (see p. 59), with red flowers and very dark red foliage is one of the best. Even more widely grown is *L. cardinalis*, with green foliage and red flowers. Of the more modern cultivars, 'Dark Crusader' is rich red, 'Compliment Scarlet' is pillar-box red while 'Russian Princess' has purple flowers and dark foliage.

Lupinus Easy to grow, colourful and flamboyant as cut flowers, it is obvious why lupins are so popular. Best on acid soils, most are now raised from seed and many will flower in the first year from an early sowing. 'Dwarf Gallery', 2 ft (60 cm), is very prolific in a good selection of colours while 'New Generation', 4 ft (1.2 m), is tall and

Lychnis coronaria 'Oculata' forms an upright silvery clump and is ideal for planting in a sunny position (see p. 62)

Although peonies are not easy to propagate, their flowers and foliage are well worth having in any border. This example is *Paeonia mlokosewitschii*

elegant with a bonus of retaining its lowest flowers until the topmost ones are open. The colour range is wonderful but they will need staking as the spikes are so long and heavy.

Lychnis Rather a mixed bunch but all are happy in sun and any reasonable soil. They are also good for cutting. 'Dusty Miller', *L. coronaria*, 2–3 ft (60–90 cm), is easily raised from seed and will self-sow generously when happy. It thrives on a dry soil and the grey felted leaves show off the magenta flowers well. The white form and 'Oculata' (see p. 61), a pink-eyed white, are especially effective. Taller and more stiffly upright is the brilliant red *L. chalcedonica*, 3–4 ft (90 cm–1.2 m), with flat heads of small flowers; there are also examples with less attractive pink, white and double flowers.

Meconopsis Most meconopsis are better in the north and west than the drier south and east. But they are worth giving the humus-rich, acid soil and shelter from icy winds that they like for the sake the almost unbelievable blue flowers. The Welsh poppy, *M. cambrica*, 15 in. (38 cm), is the exception and will grow almost anywhere, its pale ferny-like foliage setting off the delicate yellow or orange flowers well. It can self-sow too much when happy. Of the blue poppies, *M. betonicifolia*, 3ft (90 cm), is the easiest to grow, is a good perennial when happy and is easily raised from seed. It is best divided every three or four years in September.

Monarda Bee balm or bergamot is a fine border plant, with aromatic foliage and flowers carried in tiers up the stem. It creeps well if given sunshine and moist soil though it should not be waterlogged in winter. In dry summers mildew can be a problem. Most of those available are hybrids and the brighter red 'Cambridge Scarlet', the deep purple 'Prairie Night' and the pure white 'Snowmaiden' are all good. There is also a range of mildew-resistant cultivars named after the signs of the zodiac.

Paeonia The flowers of peonies may be fleeting but they are captivating while at their best. Some gardeners prefer the simplicity of the species, others the opulence of the double hybrids. Most are happy in a rich but well-drained soil and are best left undisturbed until they show signs of deteriorating. The so-called Molly-the-witch, *P. mlokosewitschii*, 2ft (60 cm) (opposite), not only flowers early but its lemony flowers are a lovely pure shade. There is an ever expanding range of hybrids, 3 ft (90 cm), many from America, and all have the benefit of good foliage to follow the large flowers which may be single, fully double or with a mass of shorter petals in the centre. It is impossible to make a selection; I can only advise choosing from a Chelsea Flower Show display or a well-labelled garden and obtaining those that particularly catch your fancy.

Papaver Oriental poppies, 2–3 ft (60–90 cm), are nothing if not colourful, and thrive in sunshine and well-drained soil, preferably one which is not over-rich. The leaves disappear in early summer leaving an awkward gap which must be masked by a late developer. The roots go deep and are apt to re-shoot if a plant is moved. 'Black and White' has pure white flowers with a black blotch at the base of each petal. 'Mrs Perry' is a salmony pink, 'Turkish Delight' is soft pink. For more fiery shades, go for the scarlet 'Goliath'.

Phlox Border phlox like sun for most or all of the day and a rich soil that is not too dry. Their fragrance is powerful, although not everyone can smell it. The two groups are based on *P. maculata* and *P. paniculata*. The former has cylindrical flower heads made up of myriads of small flowers and is well scented. The lilac-pink 'Alpha', and 'Omega' in white with a lilac eye, are the most often seen although the pure white 'Miss Lingard' is well worth seeking out. Most cultivars derive from *P. paniculata*, and there are many. As with poppies, I recommend choosing on the basis of plants in flower, but I suggest you look out for the deep lilac 'Branklyn', 2ft (60 cm), and the dark-eyed pink 'Eva Callum', 3ft (90 cm), which are shorter than most. There are also examples with variegated foliage; 'Nora Leigh' (see p. 64) has white-edged leaves and 'Harlequin' is variegated in white and pink. The cultivars of *P. paniculata*, in par-

ticular, are subject to attack from mildew and stem eelworm, so to rejuvenate ailing clumps propagate from root cuttings rather than stem cuttings.

Polemonium Easy and quick-growing border plants, they are sometimes short lived unless divided regularly – although there are usually plenty of self-sown seedlings around. All are best in good soil, preferably in sun, and are self supporting. The familiar blue Jacob's ladder, *P. caeruleum*, 2 ft (60 cm), is a fine plant with bright flowers on upright stems above good dark foliage. *P. foliosissimum* 2 ft (60 cm), is lilac, the blue *P. reptans*, 12 in. (30 cm), is earlier and is particularly underrated, while *P. carneum*, 18 in. (45 cm), is pink.

Primula Few of this large group are suitable for general border cultivation although many will succeed given special conditions. Primroses, including doubles, are good in any borders where they will be shaded by taller perennials later in the season. Purple, lilac or white drumstick primroses, *P. denticulata*, are less fussy.

Pulmonaria The lungworts, 12 in. (30 cm), are among the most indispensable of spring plants, their flowers giving way to splendid foliage in the best forms. Good ground cover, happy in shade and tolerant of poor conditions, they nevertheless repay good cultivation. Of the spotted-leaved forms, 'Lewis Palmer' is a strong-growing rich blue and 'Fruhlingshimmel' is a lovely pale shade. 'Dora Bielefeld' is about the only good pink, 'Sissinghurst White' is the best white. 'Tim's Silver' has leaves almost entirely silvered while 'Leopard' is especially beautifully spotted. Two species are without spots, *P. angustifolia* and *P. rubra*. The best of the former is 'Blue Ensign' with large deep blue flowers while 'Redstart' and the white-streaked 'Barfield Pink' are the best of the red, early-flowering *P. rubra*.

Salvia A vast genus full of good garden plants demanding sunshine and well-drained conditions; many are not hardy in our colder counties. They are a varied lot, some with wonderful foliage, others making fine cut flowers. The tough and familiar border salvias are probably most conveniently grouped under *S. × superba*, 3 ft (90 cm) (see p. 21). 'May Night' is rich deep purple, 'Superba' is violet and has purple bracts which last well after the flowers. 'Lubecca', 18 in. (45 cm), is a good dwarf while 'Rose Queen', 2 ft (60 cm), is a fine pink form. For foliage, *S. argentea*, 3 ft (90 cm), is unbeatable, with big flat leaves covered in silvery down although unfortunately the flowers are less good. For late season flowers *S. guaranitica*, 5 ft

Phlox paniculata 'Nora Leigh' is mostly grown for its variegated foliage. The lilac-pink flowers open in summer (see p. 63)

(1.5 m), is a lovely gentian blue although it may need support, and there is the sparkling azure *S. uliginosa*, 5 ft (1.5 m), with rather sparse, waving stems. A covering of leaf litter is useful in winter.

Sedum The autumn-flowering *S. spectabile* and its hybrids, 18 in. (45 cm), are among the finest of late summer and autumn flowers and are much loved by butterflies. The flat flower heads are set off by succulent bluish foliage. They thrive in sunshine and good soil and can easily be increased by spring cuttings. 'Autumn Joy' has grey-blue leaves and is one of the later ones, with large pink heads eventually turning coppery. 'September Glow' is darker in flower and 'Iceberg' is white. 'Vera Jameson', 9 in. (23 cm) (below), has pale pink flowers but strongly purple-tinted foliage. 'Ruby Glow', 9 in. (23 cm) (below), is daintier, with small heads of pink flowers.

Symphytum Some comfreys can be very invasive; all are tough, thriving in shade and less than perfect soil. 'Hidcote Blue' and 'Hidcote Pink', both 2 ft (60 cm), are fine ground coverers but their spreading habits may be inconvenient. Equally spreading but half the height is the creamy-flowered *S. ibericum* (syn. *S. grandiflorum*), 12 in. (30 cm), with dark green leaves. The yellow-margined 'Goldsmith' is said to be a variegated form of this species but has pale blue flowers. More like a hosta at first, *S. × uplandicum* 'Variegatum' has long, oval greyish-green leaves margined in cream with tall stems of pinkish-lilac flowers. A lovely plant.

The succulent foliage of the late-flowering sedums, such as S. 'Ruby Glow', looks good long before the richly-coloured flowers open

Choosing Perennials

Short lists of perennials with different qualities and for difficult situations. For more information on those not already described in this book, there are a number of Wisley Handbooks of particular interest to enthusiasts for hardy perennials. These include *Delphiniums*, *Foliage Plants*, *The Mixed Border* and *Primroses and Auriculas*.

Acid soil
Epimedium
Gentian
Lupinus
Meconopsis
Trillium

Clay soil
Anemone × hybrida
Bergenia
Hellebore
Inula
Rodgersia

Climbers
Dicentra macrocapnos
Eccremocarpus scaber
Humulus lupulus 'Aureus'
Lathyrus
Tropaeolum speciosum

Damp shade
Ferns
Hellebore
Hosta
Polygonatum
Tricyrtis

Dry shade
Alchemilla mollis
Carex pendula
Iris foetidissima
Polystichum setifeum
Periwinkles (Vinca)

Hot and dry sites
Euphorbia characias
Zauschneria
Acanthus spinosus
Crambe maritima
Eryngium maritimum

Late flowering
Aster lateriflorus 'Horizontalis'
Helenium
Dendranthemum
   (Chrysanthemum)
   'Anastasia', 'Bronze
   Elegance'
Liriope spicata
Salvia uliginosa

Quick spreaders
Achillea millifolium hybrids
Achillea ptarmica
Anemone × hybrida
Lamium maculatum
Polygonum bistorta

Bedding
Plants

—— GRAHAM RICE ——

An eye-catching summer bedding display composed of
tagetes, dianthus, antirrhinums, asters (*Callistephus*) and
lobelia

Summer Plants

Summer bedding plants are generally frost tender and are grown to planting size under protection before being bedded out after the last frost, generally in late May or early June. Even hardy species which are to be bedded out for the summer are raised in this way. They fall into two main categories: those raised afresh from seed each year and those overwintered as plants in frost-free conditions and propagated by cuttings.

SUMMER BEDDING FROM SEED

The majority of summer bedding plants are raised from seed early in the year. They may be half hardy annuals such as zinnias, hardy annuals such as alyssum or tender perennials such as zonal pelargoniums, which are treated as half hardy annuals. All are raised by sowing seed in warmth in early spring, growing on and then hardening off before planting out in beds and borders.

Many bedding plants can be raised on a windowsill but a greenhouse and heated propagator will give them the best start.

Greenhouse

Few gardeners erect a greenhouse specifically for raising bedding plants; an existing greenhouse will usually be used. However, the one feature that would be a great advantage is a built-in partition dividing off a small area, perhaps one third of a 12 ft × 8 ft (4 × 2.5 m) greenhouse. Some greenhouse manufacturers can supply a partition to fit into an existing structure but if this is not possible a carefully fitted rigid polythene sheet will do the job. This small, partitioned area can be heated in early spring when heating is expensive, without the need to heat the whole greenhouse. A propagator can be installed and, since it is already in a slightly heated environment, will itself use less energy. A thermostatically controlled heated mat could also be used on the staging in this area.

Alongside the greenhouse, a cold frame is invaluable, especially in those last frosty nights of spring when so many plants demand protection and facilities become congested. This can be an off-the-shelf aluminium structure or, better still, a home-made frame made of insulating blocks, old railway sleepers or tongue-and-grooved boards, built as large as (or preferably larger than) needed, and topped with glass- or polythene-glazed lights.

Windowsill

Plants raised on windowsills indoors will not usually match the quality of those raised in better conditions in the greenhouse. However, once planted out they have a habit of catching up as summer growth develops. If you can tolerate propagators and pots scattered around the house, then take advantage of the differing light conditions afforded by windows of different aspects and the varying temperatures available in different rooms in the house. By moving seedlings and young plants from one place to another as they grow, and as the season warms, it is possible to minimize the effects of the low, one-sided lighting and of the dry atmosphere.

Propagator and heated mat

An electrically heated propagator is the most important item of seed-raising equipment; it should incorporate an adjustable thermostat so that the temperature can be set accurately. Many models are available, from one-seed-tray size to larger models taking half a dozen trays or as many as 60 small pots. If you grow many plants and work on a large scale, you could build your own propagating frame on the greenhouse bench, using timber sides and base, soil-warming cables with a thermostat, plus a glass- or polythene-glazed lid. Although individual seeds vary in their requirements, a temperature of 65-70°F (18-21°C) suits most.

For windowsill seed raising, long, narrow propagators specially designed to fit on a sill are available. In addition to a heated model, a couple of unheated propagators are also valuable to provide an intermediate stage between the cosy conditions in the heated propagator and the harsher world outside.

In the greenhouse, intermediate conditions are also necessary and may be provided in a number of ways. The greenhouse itself can be heated slightly, part of the greenhouse can be partitioned off and only this area heated, or a larger frame within the greenhouse can be built and maintained at an intermediate temperature. In all these cases a growing temperature of 45°F (7°C) represents the best compromise between ideal growing conditions and energy conservation. A good alternative is to install a heated mat which keeps the roots of the plants at a relatively high temperature, about 60°F (15°C), and which allows the air temperature to be kept just frost-free. This will give a net saving in energy and also encourage short bushy growth.

Pots and trays

For most gardeners it is extremely wasteful to sow seed in seed trays unless very large numbers of plants are needed. Do you really want to raise 500 antirrhinums? Plastic pots 3 in. (8 cm) or 4 in. (10 cm) across, preferably square ones, will enable you to raise all you need while being as economical of space as possible; if you do need an especially large number of some plants, sow in two or three pots. For the later stages of growth I also prefer square pots, as these not only provide the flexibility to fill every inch of space without the awkward wasteful gaps sometimes left by the seed trays, but offer individual plants more root room, so that they suffer less disturbance when planted out. I tend to grow small quantities of a large range of plants, but if you prefer to raise large numbers of relatively few genera, pricking out into trays is probably more sensible.

If you use trays, the extra root room provided by deep trays is invaluable; the plants will be of better quality, while the extra compost gives them a larger water reserve, invaluable if you go away for the weekend and the weather turns hot. Although such trays are more expensive, they are usually made of stouter materials, so last longer.

Recently, I have found propagating trays a very useful alternative. These plastic trays are divided into small cells, each of which accommodates one young plant. Seed is sown individually or in pinches in the small-sized cells and then each plug of compost with its germinated seedlings is moved to a larger cell or pot with no root disturbance. This minimizes root damage and prevents setbacks in growth.

Compost

Loam-based and soil-less composts can be used to raise bedding plants but each has its own special requirements. Try to avoid using more than one type at a time as this makes it more difficult to give each the care it needs. I avoid loam-based composts for bedding plants as the quality is very unpredictable, and a poor loam-based compost is difficult to improve. Soil-less composts are less variable and also lighter in weight, and bedding plants grow well in them. Coir composts and other peat substitutes vary noticeably from brand to brand. My advice is to stick to one brand and get used to it. The one thing all coir composts seem to have in common is that the surface dries out quickly while underneath the compost remains moist, so careful watering is necessary.

Cineraria 'Silver Dust' (see p.87) and fibrous-rooted begonias can both be raised from seed, although the seed of the begonias is very fine

SOWING TECHNIQUES

Tip out some seed compost from its bag on to your potting bench (or polythene-covered kitchen table!), fluff it up and make sure it is moist but not soggy. Ensure that the pots for seed sowing are clean and gather together everything else you will need: clingfilm or glass, plus newspaper for covering seed pots, a watering can with a fine rose, labels and marker pen, and a presser.

If you are sowing more than just one or two genera, start by filling pots about half a dozen at a time. Fill each pot loosely to the brim, wipe off the surplus level with the rim of the pot then tap the pot on the bench to settle the compost; finally, firm very gently to level the surface, using a home-made presser. A presser can be made from a round of plywood or anything about the right size to fit inside a 3 in. (8 cm) pot with angular rather than rounded edges; a plastic beaker is sometimes suitable. The surface of the compost should be about ¼ in. (6 mm) below the rim of the pot. Now open your first seed packet, remove the smaller inner foil packet inside, cut the top off with scissors and inspect the contents.

Consider now how many plants you need to grow and decide whether to sow all the seed or just some of it, whether it will all go in one seed pot or whether you need another. It is difficult to advise on exactly how much seed to sow in each pot as some seeds are so much bigger than others. But bear in mind that although a pot will take more begonia seedlings than zinnia seeds, the temptation to fill a pot with large numbers of tiny begonias or lobelias should be resisted.

The seed must be sown thinly and evenly over the surface of the compost. For all but the largest seed I find that the best method is as follows. Having cut the top off the inner packet, make a crease half-way along one of the cut edges. Hold the packet between the thumb and middle finger, tip the packet slightly so that the seed tends to run into the crease, then tap the edge of the packet with index finger to encourage the seed to roll off the edge and on to the compost. This way you can see exactly how much seed is falling on to the compost, and by moving the packet back and forth as the seed falls, the surface can be covered evenly.

Larger seeds such as marigolds and dahlias need less careful sowing and can be redistributed over the surface of the compost after sowing by moving them with the point of a pencil. Very small seeds like those of lobelias, petunias and begonias can be tricky, but the method I have described will distribute the seed evenly, although this is less easy if your eyesight is poor. The old trick of adding a small amount of very dry silver sand to the seed, mixing thoroughly and sowing the highly visible mixture, works well. Large seeds can be sown in twos in individual pots, thinned to one as they develop and then potted on before planting out.

After sowing, most seed needs a covering of compost, although plants with small seeds like begonias and petunias can simply be pressed gently into the surface of the compost. Over the years I have found that this gentle pressing is very useful, reducing the amount of fine compost that needs sifting over the seed to a covering as deep as the seed itself. Some gardeners use an old kitchen sieve for this purpose but I find this is too fine and use a home-made sieve made by tacking a square of greenhouse shade netting to a light wooden frame. Vermiculite can also be used as a seed covering but is less easy to manage than compost. Immediately after sowing, write the label giving the name, source of seed and date of sowing.

AFTER SOWING

The pots now need watering. I prefer to water gently with a fine rose on a watering can, tipping it to get water flowing before spraying the pots, then moving it away before stopping – this avoids huge drips disturbing the seeds. Or the pots could be stood in water so that it soaks up from below until the compost surface darkens. In either case, add a copper fungicide to the water to help prevent damping off.

When surplus water has drained away, the pots can go into the propagator. Most seeds do not need any more darkness to encourage germination than is provided by the compost over them, but they do need a clear, moisture-retentive covering – fine, uncovered seed is in danger of drying out. This can be a rectangle of glass for trays or rounds of glass or rigid plastic or clingfilm for individual pots. However, for most seeds, if the lid is on the propagator, and it is covered with paper to exclude sun and is not placed in a sunny position then no additional cover is needed, although careful misting or gentle watering may sometimes be necessary.

Seeds should then be checked twice a day and, as soon as germination occurs, remove any paper covering and the glass or plastic a day or two later. Pots are now best removed to a slightly cooler temperature where the seedlings can grow on until the seed leaves have expanded. Water regularly, adding a copper fungicide as a precaution against damping off.

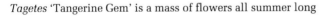

Tagetes 'Tangerine Gem' is a mass of flowers all summer long

PRICKING OUT

The usual advice is to prick out seedlings 'when large enough to handle'. For most plants, this stage is reached when the first pair of leaves, the seed leaves, are well developed.

Water the seed pot well with fungicide a few hours beforehand and moisten the potting compost. Make sure pots or boxes, dibber and presser are clean. Fill the pots as before, although there is no need to firm with the presser.

Remove some seedlings from the pot, using the dibber or an old fork, or tip the entire contents carefully onto the bench. Make a hole in the centre of the pot, deep and wide enough to take the full length of the root without breaking it. Gently extract a seedling, place it in the hole with its seed leaves just above soil level, and tap the pot sharply on the bench to settle the soil around the roots. This, followed by watering, settles the compost well without compacting it too much. Over-firmed compost can lead to waterlogging and rot and is the main cause of failures.

Trays are filled in a similar way although it pays to half-fill the tray and press the compost carefully into the corners and along the edges before topping up and striking off the surplus. Here, a purpose-made presser may be useful but, again, only gentle firming is required.

The number of seedlings pricked out into each tray depends on the size of the tray and the vigour of the plant. A standard seed tray would generally take 24. Make evenly spaced holes with the dibber along one long and one short side and plant the seedlings as before. Use these rows as a guide and prick out the rest of the seedlings. Tap the box down and water well with a copper fungicide.

CARE TO PLANTING TIME

After pricking out, the pots or boxes do not require as high a temperature as was needed for seed germination; nevertheless, a relatively high temperature, even for just a few days, helps root growth to start promptly. I stand my pricked-out seedlings on a heated mat giving a root temperature of 60°F (15°C), with a minimum air temperature of 45°F (7°C). In fact, with care in watering and attention to good ventilation and disease prevention, night air temperatures of just above freezing will still produce good plants.

Cosmos 'Sonata White' (see p.88) with pelargoniums and marigolds planted out in blocks in a special display bed

I find that the stage when the seedlings are moved off the mat and on to the open bench is generally governed not so much by choosing the optimum stage of growth, but by the need to find space on the mat for the next batch. Most gardeners are limited for greenhouse space and even the addition of high level shelves and the utilization of the space below the benches may not provide enough scope for moving the plants to the next stage at the very best moment. Fortunately, bedding plants are tough and adaptable and can usually cope with less than perfect conditions as long as growing techniques are adapted accordingly.

Some plants like antirrhinums, calceolarias, gazanias and other almost-hardy plants are best grown as cool as possible to encourage branching and prevent lanky growth. They will do best if kept just frost free.

For most people, the space problem is at its most acute at the stage when the plants are developing well and in need of spacing out, whilst still requiring protection from the last spring frosts. This is the hardening-off stage when plants are acclimatized to the outside world after being cosseted in artificially warm conditions for the first months of their life.

For windowsill gardeners, the sill of an unheated spare room in the house may be a convenient spot for a period, followed perhaps by a windowsill in the garage. There may be space for a small cold frame in the garden for the final stage or plants can be moved outside during the day and moved back to the garage when frost threatens; or they could be left in a sheltered porch.

For gardeners with more facilities, a cold frame is the answer, and the bigger the better, hence the earlier suggestion of a home-made frame. Some cold frames are so expensive that a cheap aluminium greenhouse seems a better buy. But whether you use a cold frame or cold greenhouse for hardening off, the idea is to expose the young plants increasingly to outside conditions by reducing their protection. This is done by opening vents or removing frame lights on blue-sky days, then on chillier days, while closing them at night when frost threatens or in spells of cold wind or heavy rain. For the last couple of weeks before planting, the plants should have the maximum possible exposure to the weather.

During this period the young plants should never be allowed to dry out and should be fed every 10-14 days, depending on the weather, with a general purpose liquid fertilizer. They should also be protected from slugs and inspected regularly for other pests and diseases. Most modern cultivars are bred to branch well from low down to create a bushy plant without the need for pinching out, but older kinds may need their tips pinched out and this should be done when the plants are relatively small. In general, I am against routine pinching, and prefer to rely on giving the individual plants sufficient space for their natural branching to develop.

PLANTING OUT

Although most bedding plants are generally fairly tough and adaptable, good soil preparation pays off. In soil of good fertility, loosening the soil with a border fork to the full depth of the tines and removing weeds is often enough. The soil should then be trodden well and a dressing of 2-4 oz (55-110 g) per square yard or metre of a general fertilizer such as blood, fish and bone or Growmore raked in before planting. When bedding plants are grown on their own in beds reserved for temporary displays, annual additions of organic matter, such as rotted manure or garden compost, are invaluable. Whether you dig this in before planting the summer bedding, or in the autumn before planting spring bedding, will depend on your soil: apply it in autumn to

A window box full of summer bedding – petunias, lobelia, pelargoniums –
none tall enough to darken the room

heavy clay soils and in spring to lighter sandy soils.

When bedding plants are set in small groups in mixed borders, the degree of preparation required for individual planting sites will depend on the overall fertility of the soil. If the border has recently been replanted and plenty of organic matter dug in, a sprinkling of 2 oz (55 g) fertilizer per square yard or metre will suffice. If it is some years since this was done, then forking in well-rotted compost or one of the peat substitutes followed by fertilizer at double the rate may be more appropriate. Where individual plants are set out in a mixed border, I use a planting mix made up of a two-gallon bucket of old potting or seed compost mixed with 2 oz (55 g) of fertilizer, and this is worked into the soil immediately before planting.

Plants must be moist when planted and I like to give them a final liquid feed a few hours beforehand. Plants from pots are planted with a trowel, those from trays are best removed in one block and then separated by pulling them apart. After planting and firming in well, water them again individually with liquid feed to ensure that there are readily available nutrients for the new roots to utilize.

A to Z of Plants
Raised from Seed

This descriptive list of the most important seed-raised bedding plants is intended to give an idea of the impressive range now available, to select especially good cultivars from the thousands on offer and to give advice on any special requirements they may have. Seed packets now give increasingly comprehensive instructions and should be consulted before sowing.

Ageratum Clusters of fluffy flowers in various blues, pinks and white. Although blue ageratums reproduce badly in pictures in seed catalogues, in general they make better plants than those with pink flowers, and white flowers tend to brown as they die. Good smaller cultivars for edging and the front of the border are the spreading 'Blue Swords', 8 in. (20 cm), mid blue, the more compact and purplish 'North Sea', 8 in. (20 cm), and the larger-leaved, azure 'Blue Mink', 9 in. (23 cm). 'Southern Cross', 10 in. (25 cm), is a lovely blue and white bicolour while 'Pinky', 8 in. (20 cm), and 'Summer Snow', 8 in. (20 cm), give pink and white. Tall types for the back of the border and for cutting include 'Blue Horizon', 2 ft (60 cm), and the white 'Highness', 2 ft (60 cm).

Do not cover the seed, simply press it into the compost and prick out into pots if possible.

Alyssum (*Lobularia maritima*) Flat carpeting plants in white, various pinks, lilacs and purples; the darker colours are generally less vigorous than the white. 'Snow Crystals', 4 in (10 cm), is a neat, large-flowered, well-scented white while 'Carpet of Snow', 4 in. (10 cm), spreads to 15 in. (38 cm). 'Rosie O'Day' is a good pink, 'Wonderland' the best purple, and 'Creamery' a new pale cream shade. Pastel Carpet and Morning Mist are good mixtures.

Although alyssum can be grown as a hardy annual it is often raised as a bedding plant. Prick out seedlings of mixtures in threes to get the best tapestry effect. Do not overwater in boxes and watch for grey mould (*Botrytis*).

Antirrhinum Commonly known as snapdragon, these are now

Impatiens (see p.89) are ideal plants for shady places. This New Guinea hybrid has strongly variegated foliage available in a wide range of sizes and colours. Unfortunately rust is a problem and no varieties are completely resistant. The best mixtures with the usual, two-lipped flowers include Floral Carpet and Tahiti, 8-10 in. (20-25 cm), Coronette, Monarch and Sonnet, 15-18 in. (38-45 cm), and Giant Forerunner, 3 ft (1 m). Doubles include Sweetheart, 12 in. (30 cm) and Madame Butterfly, 2½ ft (75 cm), open-throated types include Little Darling, 12 in. (30 cm) (see p. 126) and Trumpet Serenade, 18 in. (45 cm). Brighton Rock, 18 in. (45 cm), is the first of the reintroduced Victorian striped antirrhinums. Some of the finest antirrhinums are single colours in the medium height range and these include 'Black Prince' with bronze leaves and deep purple flowers, 'Lavender Monarch', and 'Princess Purple and White', a lovely bicolour.

Grow cool to promote branching and beware of damping off. Spray all cultivars regularly, even those said to be rust resistant, with propiconazole. Cut back plants after flowering and water well to promote a second flush of flowers.

Aster (*Callistephus chinensis*) Relatively late-flowering plants once used mainly for cutting; dwarfer forms are now available for bedding. Wilt is an incurable soil disease which attacks asters grown in the same soil for too long; and none are completely resistant. A wide variety of flower forms is available including singles, chrysanthemum-flowered, ostrich-feathered, quilled, incurved, pompon and crested. Mixtures for edging and the front of the border include the incurved Milady, 10 in. (25 cm), the lovely quilled Teisa Stars, 10 in. (25 cm), and the small ostrich-feathered Comet, 8 in. (20 cm). Good taller mixtures include the single Andrella, 2½ ft (75 cm), Pompon, 18 in. (45 cm), which includes bicolours and tricolours, the chrysanthemum-flowered Riviera, 2 ft (60 cm), and the incurved Duchess, 2 ft (60 cm).

Beware of damping off, prick out taller types into individual pots if possible. To obtain a reasonable display on wilt-infected soil, pot on plants into 5 in. (13 cm) pots to give them a reservoir of uninfected soil. Remember that asters start into flower later than most bedders, so site them accordingly.

Begonia Begonias for bedding fall into two groups. Large-flowered tuberous-rooted begonias have flamboyant double flowers in a wide range of colours while small-flowered, fibrous-rooted begonias have single flowers in a more restricted range. Seed of tuberous begonias is more expensive so they are often preferred for containers and they usually come only in mixtures.

The well-known tuberous Non Stop, 9 in. (23 cm), comes in ten colours and now has a bronze-leaved cousin, Non Stop Ornament.

Aster Pompon (see opposite) is one of the taller growing selections suitable for planting in a mixed border

Musical, 9 in. (23 cm), in four colours, has a more trailing habit while the semi-double Chanson in five shades is a genuine trailer. 'Pin-Up', 9 in. (23 cm) (see p.88), is a single white with a pink picotee. Fibrous-rooted begonias come in green-leaved and bronze-leaved types, with flowers in the red/pink/white range; most are compact and bushy although a few have a trailing habit. Again most come as mixtures and for mixes including those with green and bronzed leaves try Lucia, 8 in. (20 cm), (Devon Gems and New Generation are similar), or the larger-flowered Party Fun, 12 in. (30 cm). Olympia, 8 in. (20 cm), is a good green-leaved mix, Cocktail, 8 in. (20 cm) is a good bronze-leaved mix. Individual colours worth considering include 'Coco Ducolor', 12 in. (30 cm), with bronze leaves and pink-edged white flowers, 'Danica Red', 10 in. (25 cm), with bronze leaves and scarlet flowers and the trailing green-leaved 'Pink Avalanche'.

Leave uncovered after sowing but keep humidity high by covering with clingfilm, water from below and keep the temperature at 70°F (21°C) or above if possible. Beware of damping off. Plant in rich soil. The fibrous types in particular will take partial shade.

Cineraria (*Senecio bicolor* subsp. *cineraria*) Silver-leaved plants for foliage borders or among flowering plants; a good foil for many other plants and may overwinter in mild seasons. 'Silver Dust', 9 in. (23 cm) (see p. 77), has deeply cut foliage while 'Cirrus', 12 in. (30cm), is an oak-leaved type with lobed leaves. Easy to raise.

'Pin-Up' is a showy tuberous-rooted begonia with an upright growth habit (see p.87)

Cosmos Vigorous plants with attractive finely cut foliage and large, single daisy flowers all summer. All are good in bedding and for cutting. The mixtures come in various reds, pinks and white with some bicolours. Sensation, 3-4 ft (1-1.2 m), is the standard mixture while Sonata, 2 ft (60 cm), is the best dwarf type. The lovely Sea Shells, 3 ft (1 m), has the petals rolled into fluted tubes. Among the single colours, 'Sonata White', 18 in. (45 cm) (see p. 81) and 'Purity', 3-4 ft (1-1.2 m), both white, are stunning, as is the pink-eyed white 'Daydream', 3-4 ft (1-1.2 m).

Easy to raise, cosmos are vigorous and are best pricked out into individual pots. In the garden they make bushy plants and may need support in windy areas. Dead head or cut for the house regularly. Can be sown *in situ* in May.

Dahlia It is only worth raising dwarfer dahlias from seed; the taller large-flowered dahlias are better grown from tubers. Dahlias will often be in flower when planted and then continue until the frosts. Usually available only in mixtures, a few single colours are now being listed. Coltness Hybrids, 18 in. (45 cm), are single flowered in a wide range of shades, Unwins Dwarf Hybrids, 2 ft (60 cm) is a fine semi-double mix and Dandy, 2ft (60 cm), has a collar of quilled petals around the eye; Figaro, 12 in. (30 cm), is the best dwarf. Redskin, 18 in. (45 cm), and Diablo, 12 in. (30 cm), are bronze-leaved mixtures, although their flowers tend to be rather watery in colour.

Easy to raise and will germinate well at 60°F (15°C), then best pricked out into individual pots when they can be grown on very cool. Beware of aphids. Lift any plants you especially like and store the tubers.

Dianthus The best bedding dianthus are colourful and long flowering but some are far too dumpy and are better as pot plants. They come in carnation types and those which are more like single pinks. Of the carnation types Knight, 12 in. (30 cm), is a good dwarf mixture but few colours are scented, the powerfully fragrant Giant Chabaud Mixed, 2 ft (60 cm), is wonderful in a large bed while 'Scarlet Luminette', 2ft. (60 cm), is a sparkling colour for borders or cutting. Ideal, 12 in. (30 cm), Telstar, 9 in. (23 cm), and Princess, 9 in. (23 cm), are all fine mixtures with good colours while as individual shades try the blood-red 'Telstar Crimson', 9 in. (23 cm), 'Snow Fire', 9 in. (23 cm), in white with a scarlet eye, and 'Colour Magician', 9 in. (23 cm), which opens white and fades to deep pink.

Best sown in a seed compost rather than multi-purpose compost as dianthus dislike high nutrient levels. Grow cool to encourage bushiness and plant out in full sun or partial shade. Prolonged drought may curtail flowering. All, in fact, are perennials and may overwinter in well-drained conditions.

Gazania Flamboyant low-growing plants with daisy flowers in many sunny shades, some also have silvery foliage. The flowers stay closed on cool, dull days but are stunning in sunnier conditions. The dwarf Mini-Star, 8 in. (20 cm), has a wide range of colours and the white and yellow may be available separately. Talent, 8 in. (20 cm), is similar but has grey foliage while Sundance, 12 in. (30 cm), has much larger flowers at 4 in. (10 cm) across, many of them striped, and is good for cutting.

Easy to raise and can be grown cool after pricking out, gazanias are also hardier than most bedders so can be planted out a little earlier. Always plant in full sun; shelter is an advantage.

Geranium see **Pelargonium**

Impatiens The popular busy lizzies are adaptable plants in an impressive range of shades and a vast number of cultivars. Impatiens are the best bedders for shady positions but may flower poorly in hot, dry conditions. Eventual height depends greatly on growing conditions, shade and moisture producing the tallest plants.

The best mixtures, in ascending order of eventual plant height, are Super Elfin, 6-8 in. (15-20 cm), Accent, Expo, Tempo and Blitz, 12-15 in. (30-38 cm). Super Elfin has the biggest colour range, Blitz has the largest flowers. Super Elfin Pearl, 6-8 in. (15-20 cm), is a stunning pastel mixture, Eye Eye, 8 in. (20 cm), is a lovely mixture of eyed cultivars, and Starbright, 8 in. (20 cm), is a mixture of colours with white stars. Rosette will give a good proportion of doubles. Spectra is a large-flowered mixture of New Guinea hybrids, many with variegated foliage (see p. 84). Separate colours are available from many of these mixtures and I would recommend the unique 'Tempo Burgundy', the picotee 'Super Elfin Swirl', the stunning 'Expo White' and the exceptionally floriferous 'Salmon Profusion', 9 in. (23 cm).

Sow in a well-drained seed compost, press the seed into the surface and do not cover; keep humid. Water with tepid water and feed sparingly. Prick out before true leaves develop, reduce temperatures gradually for growing on and harden off gently. Busy Lizzies react poorly to sudden changes of conditions.

Lobelia The bush and trailing types are our most popular blue-flowered bedders but are now available in an increasing variety of other shades. Expect a few blues amongst the whites. Bush types reach about 6 in. (15 cm); 'Crystal Palace' is the darkest with slightly bronzed foliage, 'Mrs Clibran' is dark with a white eye, 'Cambridge Blue' is paler. There is also 'Rosamund' in purplish red and 'White Lady'. Many mixtures are available but Kaleidoscope has the best range. Among trailers the white-eyed 'Sapphire' is the darkest blue while 'Light Blue Fountain' is sky blue; there are also the more or less self explanatory 'Ruby Cascade', 'Lilac Fountain' and 'Rose Fountain'. In mixtures Fountain is especially floriferous and not too straggly while giving the most diverse range of colours.

Surface sow thinly and cover with clingfilm to keep moist. Prick out in small patches of seedlings and grow cool once established to improve bushiness. Beware of damping off.

Marigold There are three kinds of marigolds: French, African and hybrids between the two. The French are generally smaller in habit and flower size, have single or double flowers and are available in yellows, golds, oranges, chestnut and mahogany shades and in various combinations. The Africans have dense, fully double flowers and are medium or tall with flowers in a narrower yellow/gold/orange range. The Afro-French hybrids tend to be medium in height, single or double, and mainly in the African colours.

The best single-flowered French marigolds are the Mischief, 12 in. (30 cm), series, available as a mixture and single colours, while for something shorter try Espagna, 8-10 in. (20-25 cm). 'Red

Marietta', 8 in. (20 cm), in mahogany-red edged in orange is one of a number of colours available separately. In doubles good mixtures are Boy-O-Boy, 6 in. (15 cm), and Sophia, 10 in. (25 cm), with the brilliant coloured 'Yellow Jacket', 8 in. (20 cm), and the unique 'Safari Tangerine', 9 in. (23 cm), both good separates. In recent years African marigolds have become shorter and larger flowered, but are still only available in yellow, gold and orange. Inca, Perfection and Discovery are all good dwarf, large-flowered mixtures with some colours available individually. They can all look rather squashed and dumpy and may suffer in wet weather although they are good in containers. Gay Ladies, 15 in. (38 cm), and Crackerjack, 3 ft (1 m), suffer less in bad weather and look better in the garden. The primrose-yellow 'Doubloon', 2½ ft (75 cm), is a good separate. Afro-French marigolds set no seed and so are very prolific and need no dead heading. Zenith, 10 in. (25 cm), is a wonderful double-flowered mix as is the slightly taller Solar, 14 in. (35 cm), with the mahogany 'Seven Star Red', 12 in. (30 cm), an outstanding separate colour. 'Susie Wong', 12 in. (30 cm), is a good lemony single.

All marigolds have large seeds which are easy to sow and they grow quickly so can be sown late to minimize on heat. The Africans are best pricked out into individual pots and planted before they start to flower. Plant all marigolds in full sun and dead head regularly to prolong flowering; this also improves the appearance of dwarf Africans significantly.

Mimulus Relatively new as a bedding plant, now available in a variety of sizes and a wide range of sparkling colours. Very quick to flower from seed so ideal as an emergency filler. Malibu, 6 in. (15 cm), is being superseded by Magic, 6 in. (15 cm), in a wider range of colours, including bicolours, while Calypso, 9 in. (23 cm), has large spotted flowers in a wide range. 'Viva', 12 in. (30 cm), is bright yellow with red spots. Sow late, grow cool, plant in sun or partial shade and do not allow to become too dry. If drought curtails flowering, soak well and clip over lightly.

Nemesia Now enjoying a revival, nemesias come in an enchanting range of mixtures and separate colours, in large- and small-flowered forms. They are at their best in cooler parts of the country. Carnival, 9-12 in. (23-30 cm), is a large-flowered, brightly coloured mixture, Tapestry (Pastel), 9 in. (23 cm) (see p. 112), is smaller flowered with softer colours. 'Blue Bird', 9 in. (23 cm), is a small-flowered, white-eyed blue. The fluffy seed can be difficult to sow evenly. Sow cool and grow on steadily, for nemesias dislike high temperatures. Plant out in partial shade, or full sun

An appealing combination of purple-flowered *Nicotiana* Sensation, *Chlorophytum elatum* 'Vittatum' and variegated ivies

with moist soil. Comes into flower early and may burn out by midsummer, although very colourful in the meantime.

Nicotiana These lovely evening-scented flowers come as tall border and dwarf bedding cultivars. Sensation, 3 ft (1 m), is a beautifully scented mix in a wide range of clear colours and bicolours. *N. affinis*, 3 ft (1 m), is a powerfully scented pure white, though the flowers may close temporarily in the heat of day. 'Unwins Lime Green', 2 ft (60 cm), is a very strongly coloured lime-green. Domino, 12 in. (30 cm), is the best short type with seven colours, some available separately, including picotees. Sow on the surface and press into compost; relatively quick growing so grow cool. Look out for whitefly and leafhoppers. Plant in full sun.

Pelargonium Popular and long-flowering zonal pelargoniums available in a bewildering range, giving colour all summer. Seed is expensive but modern cultivars are extraordinarily free flowering. A few display dramatic leaf zoning. They can be divided into standards, with relatively small numbers of large flower heads packed with florets, and floribundas, with a large number of smaller heads, each with fewer florets; both these groups reach 12-15 in. (30-38 cm). There are also those particularly suitable for growing in various containers.

Century, Horizon, Sundance and Gala are all excellent mixtures of the traditional type with many colours available separately, while Pastorale and Torbay Colour Mix are good, less expensive mixtures. There are some lovely separate colours available and I would pick out 'Orange Appeal', a real orange though rather weak, 'Picasso', a purple with an orange eye, the white-eyed pink 'Hollywood Star', the pale pink 'Apple Blossom Orbit' and 'Gala White'. In the floribunda types Multibloom, Avanti and the distinctive Sensation with vast numbers of rather open flower heads, are all impressive mixtures. Again, many individual colours are available, with 'Lucky Break' a good low-cost alternative. Container types include the very compact Video mix, 8 in. (20 cm), for window boxes and small tubs, and for baskets and large tubs the strong-growing 'Breakaway Red' and 'Breakaway Salmon', with spreading habit.

Germinate at 75°F (24°C) if possible until after emergence, then prick out into cells for growing on cooler before potting up individually. Will usually recover from less than ideal treatment after planting. Plant in rich soil in a sunny spot and dead head regularly to promote flowering; this is especially important in the floribunda types.

Petunia Favourite bedders and container plants for their wide range of colours and free-flowering habit, although they can be poor in dull and wet summers. Three main types are available but the distinctions are becoming increasingly blurred and even the seed companies seem confused about where to place some cultivars! Multifloras have large numbers of relatively small flowers; grandifloras branch less strongly, have rather fewer flowers but may be up to 4 in. (10 cm) across; floribundas have large quantities of relatively large flowers. Very few of these are scented, so if scent is a priority an F_2 or open-pollinated mix is most likely to provide it.

The multifloras, 9 in. (23 cm), are good as bedders. The Carpet series is exceptional in its low habit, resistance to grey mould and recovery after rain. It now outclasses the old favourite Resisto series although 'Resisto Rose' is still outstanding in poor summers. The curiously named Plum Pudding is a fine-veined mix. Mirage is the best floribunda, 12 in. (30 cm), and probably the best of all petunias for bedding with its large flowers in generous quantities and its impressive recovery after bad weather. It also features some stunning individual colours. Celebrity runs it close. The grandifloras, 12 in. (30 cm), are not good in poor weather and are best as patio or basket plants where they can benefit from a little shelter. Supercascade is a stunning mix with very large flowers and a slightly trailing habit, 'Supercascade Lilac' ('Birthday Celebration') is an outstanding separate colour. The Supermagic series has darker colours. Hulahoop is a very dramatic white-edged mix while the Daddy series are all strongly veined. Doubles, 12-15 in. (30-38 cm), need even more shelter than the grandifloras although the Duo mix is less fully double and does better in the open. In conservatories Double Delight and the purple and white 'Purple Pirouette' are very impressive.

Sow thinly and uncovered, prick out carefully and grow cool to encourage branching. Prick out those for containers into individual pots, space others well in trays. Look out for aphids. Petunias will tolerate relatively dry conditions, so plant in full sun.

Phlox A unfashionable bedder but much improved in recent years; new cultivars are less straggly and have a better colour range. Of the large-flowered types, Hazy Days, 9 in. (23 cm), has the best range of colours while Palona, 9 in. (23 cm), is more bushy. Of the small-flowered ones, Twinkles, 6 in. (15 cm), is a white-eyed, frilly-edged mixture. Sow in well-drained compost, germinate and grow cool and beware of damping off. Plant in a sunny spot.

Salvia As well as the familiar short scarlet salvias there are two other more elegant types worth growing. Traditional salvias are

The neat plants of *Phlox* Hazy Days showing the selection of clear bright colours available

also now available in a wider range of colours. Among these, 'Red Riches', 12 in. (30 cm), is a splendid scarlet and with deep green foliage, and 'Blaze of Fire', 12 in. (30 cm), a more economical though rather variable alternative. 'Rambo', 2 ft (60 cm), is taller and more spreading. 'Phoenix Purple', 12 in. (30 cm), is a lovely rich shade while Phoenix Mixed, 12 in. (30 cm), contains purple, white, lilac and two salmon shades as well as scarlet. Pharaoh, 15 in. (38 cm), is an unusual bicoloured mixture. More unusual still is *S. farinacea* 'Victoria', 18 in. (45 cm), with narrow deep blue spikes over grey-green leaves, while *S. coccinea* 'Lady in Red', 18 in. (45 cm), is bushy and less formal in habit than traditional red salvias.

Sow uncovered but ensure high humidity, for without warm, moist conditions germination may be poor. Prick off into individual pots if possible and grow on warm at first, feeding regularly, and harden off carefully. *S. farinacea* and *S. coccinea* are less fussy.

Tagetes Dome-shaped plants with finely cut, scented foliage and vast quantities of small single flowers. Colours are typified by the following: 'Lemon Gem', 'Golden Gem', 'Tangerine Gem' and the rusty red 'Paprika', all 9 in. (23 cm). Starfire is a good mixture. Easy to raise in the same way as French marigolds.

Verbena Increasingly popular plants, slowly overcoming the problems of poor germination and mildew. Most seed-raised plants are much more compact than those raised from cuttings (p.111), all reaching about 9 in. (23 cm). Romance is a sparkling white-eyed mixture but some of the individual colours are especially attractive. 'Blue Lagoon' is deep blue with no eye, 'Showtime Belle' is rich purplish-pink, 'Peaches and Cream' opens coral-pink then fades almost to white. To get the best germination, soak the compost with fungicide the day before sowing, sow thinly and cover with grit or vermiculite. Do not then water until germination. Prick out into cells or individual pots if possible.

Zinnia Very showy plants becoming increasingly popular following hot summers but disappointing in wet seasons. There are two types, tall or bushy with large flowers, and small flowers with a more spreading habit. Belvedere, 12 in. (30 cm), is a mixture which has done well in most summers while Ruffles, 2 ft (60 cm), has especially large flower heads. 'Envy', 2 ft (60 cm) (see p. 97), is an unusual green shade. Of the smaller-flowered types, Persian Carpet, 15 in. (38 cm), is a lovely mix of bicoloured double flowers while 'Orange Star' ('Classic'), 9 in. (23 cm), is a good single orange, 'Ivory', 12 in. (30 cm), a single white.

Sow late, germinate warm but do not overwater. Prick out early into cells or pots and continue to keep on the dry side. Zinnias have a tendency to rot at soil level but cautious watering combined with drenches of a copper fungicide should keep it at bay. Plant out in full sun, water thoroughly, then leave to establish without further watering.

Other summer bedders As well as these, the most popular seed-raised bedding plants for summer, there is a huge range of other attractive summer bedders. Bedding **calceolarias** with their tiny yellow slippers flower all summer; 'Midas', 12 in. (30 cm), is a good cultivar which can be grown cool but may need an occasional dose of sequestered iron. For window boxes and baskets the trailing *Campanula isophylla* is very useful and Stella in both blue and white is ideal, although the seed is small and expensive. Good **heliotropes** are now available from seed and the dwarf 'Mini-Marine', 15 in. (38 cm), has metallic blue foliage and dark blue flowers plus a fine scent; other cultivars are slow to flower and rather straggly.

A number of new **matricarias (*Tanacetum parthenium*)** have appeared recently; 'Butterball', 9 in. (23 cm), is creamy yellow and

Salpiglossis Casino on trial at the Royal Horticultural Society's Gardens at Wisley

Zinnia 'Envy' (see p.95) has flowers of an unusal colour which, if used carefully, can add drama to a bedding scheme

the white 'Snow Crown', 18 in. (45 cm), has tight white flowers with a ring of small petals. In hot, dry situations **mesembryanthemums** always perform well, while **nolanas** are valuable spreaders for beds and containers; 'Bluebird', 6 in. (15 cm), is pale blue with a yellow throat. **Pansies** are best as winter and spring bedders but most will also do well in summer, especially in cool seasons. The Imperial series, 9 in. (23 cm), are bred for summer and come in very distinctive colours such as 'Imperial Silver Princess', a pink-eyed cream, and 'Imperial Gold Princess', a red-eyed yellow. For foliage ***Ricinus***, the castor oil plant, is easy to raise and quick growing; 'Impala', 3 ft (1 m), has large, reddish-bronze, sycamore-like foliage. **Rudbeckias** may come in marigold colours but the double-flowered 'Goldilocks' and the rusty-brown 'Rustic Dwarfs' are taller and less squat. The RHS trial at Wisley showed that **salpiglossis** is a fine summer bedder; Casino, 12 in. (30 cm), is especially good outside and can be raised in the same way as petunias.

Tender Perennials
from Cuttings

In recent years there has been a revival in the use of those tender perennials which are suitable for growing outside in the summer months, and a growing awareness of the range of plants suitable for this purpose. Abutilons, argyranthemums, gazanias, foliage helichrysums and verbenas are now much more widely seen than even five years ago, old-fashioned favourites have been rediscovered, new ones like scaevolas introduced; many have proved especially useful in containers.

These plants have a number of positive features. Whether their habit is bushy or trailing, many make substantial plants – an attractive feature at a time when there is a trend for seed-raised plants to be increasingly dumpy. They also tend to have a great deal more style than those raised from seed. The majority flower right through the summer, often starting before planting out time and sometimes continuing into December, giving unsurpassed garden value. Most are vigorous and easy to grow, usually thriving in a variety of conditions.

The one drawback is that they must be overwintered in frost-free conditions. With a few exceptions, they are easy to raise from cuttings but they still need frost protection over the winter months. Some can sit on the windowsill indoors, while mature specimens of others will flower in the conservatory right through the winter. But if you only want a few for hanging baskets or tubs, it is best simply to buy fresh plants each spring.

If you intend to replace your plants each spring, then you need no equipment at all; just buy your plants and put them in. You will find that even well established plants in 5 in. (13 cm) pots are excellent value for money. If you decide to overwinter stock, you will need facilities and equipment for taking and rooting cuttings, overwintering plants and growing and hardening them off – in reality much the same as is needed for raising bedding plants from seed. But you will find that if you only intend to overwinter a few, you can get by with a space on a windowsill and an unheated propagator. A thermostatically controlled heated propagator is useful for rooting cuttings, but not essential, depending on which of my suggested regimes you adopt.

PROPAGATION AND OVERWINTERING

These two subjects are best taken together, for the way you overwinter your plants depends on when you propagate. There are three main approaches to this, depending on the facilities at your disposal and the number of plants you want to overwinter. The technique of actually taking the cuttings is the same in each case, but the timing and care vary.

The tips of the shoots make the best cuttings and ideally they should be without flowers; some plants produce flowers on every shoot in which case simply pinch off both flowers and buds. Carefully pinch off the leaves on the lower half of the cutting then trim the stem to just below a leaf joint. Fill a 3½ in. (9 cm) pot with a moistened 50:50 mixture of peat-based cutting or potting compost and grit or perlite for drainage, then insert half a dozen cuttings up to their lowest leaf. Rooting hormones are not necessary.

My first regime will allow you to overwinter adequate stock of the maximum number of different species in the smallest space. This is ideal if your frost-free greenhouse space is limited. Cuttings are taken in late summer in exposed gardens or early autumn in protected areas, depending on where you live. The idea is to leave it as late as possible but still take them before the first frosts. The cuttings are rooted in a heated propagator and once rooted are removed to an unheated propagator or greenhouse at

Tip cuttings. 1 Stem cuttings should be taken from non-flowering shoots. 2 Remove the bottom leaves. 3 Insert several cuttings round the edge of a pot and water them in

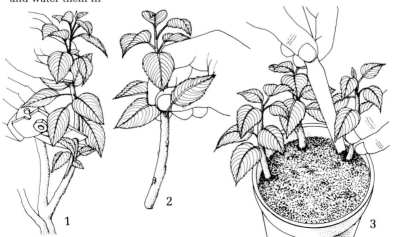

A cool combination of *Nicotiana* 'Nikki Lime' and *Abutilon pictum* 'Thompsonii'

about 45°F (7°C). They spend most of the winter, still in their pots, at a temperature maintained just above freezing, with plenty of ventilation on warm days. The aim is to keep them virtually dormant until spring with the stock of each individual species taking up the space of just one pot and with minimum energy expended on heat. Watering must be very sparing right through the winter.

In spring, there are two ways of continuing depending on the state of the cuttings by March; you can either pot them up into their own individual 3½ in. (9 cm) pots, pinch them and grow them on in the cool, or, if they have become woody and leggy, increase the temperature and the watering, then use the tips to make fresh cuttings.

My second regime requires slightly higher temperatures and allows you to overwinter fewer species in the same space, but by planting-out time you will have far more plants of each. Cuttings are taken in August or early September and after rooting are pinched out and potted into individual 3½ in. (9 cm) pots, using a standard compost. Cuttings are best taken earlier rather than later and the plants moved into 5 in. (13 cm) pots before the winter and kept growing at about 45°F (7°C). During winter, if kept just above freezing, there is an increased danger of root rot and grey mould on the foliage. In the spring the tips of all the side shoots are used as cuttings and the plants kept growing, soon yielding a fresh crop of tips for more cuttings. By planting-out time you will have a small number of large plants in 5 in. (13 cm) pots, although these would benefit from potting on if they are to be planted out, together with a large number of plants in smaller pots.

The alternative is to use windowsills, concentrate on a small number of species and take cuttings in August or September. They can be rooted in an unheated propagator or in a pot covered with a polythene bag; use a windowsill out of direct sun. Pot a couple of rooted cuttings of each species into 3½ in. (9 cm) pots and grow these on the windowsill through the winter. Take more cuttings in spring in the same way and pot these up to give vigorous young plants for setting out.

CARE TO PLANTING TIME

For a while you can manipulate the growing temperature to control the young plants' rate of growth but by late April most will be growing strongly. Many plants dislike being pot-bound and may appreciate potting on if they are filling their pots with roots long before planting time. Feeding is useful to keep plants healthy, but avoid high nitrogen feeds as this will promote sappy, delicate growth. You will find that many will be in flower well before planting out but there is no need to remove the blooms. Do not let plants become too spindly; most respond well to pinching as long as they have good light and plenty of space for side shoots to develop. Keep a watchful eye out for pests; aphids, in particular, can multiply at an alarming rate. As with seed-raised plants, hardening off is vital to ensure that young plants are sufficiently acclimatised when they are set out.

PLANTING OUT

The advice on preparation and planting given for seed-raised plants applies here as well (see p. 74). One important factor that is sometimes overlooked by gardeners used to dealing with seed-raised bedding plants is that many of these tender perennials make very substantial plants and so need much more space in which to develop during the season. Some verbenas can easily make 2 ft (60 cm) across, three times the size of their seed-raised relations, while argyranthemums 3ft (1 m) across and almost as high are not unusual in good soil. Conversely, of course, you need fewer plants to fill a given area.

A to Z of Plants
Raised from Cuttings

A stream of new cultivars and hybrids is appearing in this group of plants for the first time in many years. The names of some are very muddled; one plant may be found under a number of different names while different plants may be found under the same name; verbenas and argyranthemums suffer especially from this problem.

Abutilon There are two groups, one grown mainly for flowers and the other for foliage. Of the large-flowered types 'Golden Fleece', 4ft (1.2 m), with large yellow bells and the orange 'Firebell', 3 ft (1 m), are especially good in tubs; 'Ashford Red', 6 ft (1.8 m), and the white 'Boule de Neige', 4.6 ft (1.2-1.8 m), are more vigorous. *A. pictum* 'Thompsonii' has dark, maple-like leaves mottled in yellow with small orange flowers, while *A. megapotamicum* 'Variegatum' has oval or three-lobed, yellow-splashed leaves and small red and yellow bells. All thrive in rich conditions and full sun and also make good conservatory plants in winter, though susceptible to whitefly.

Argyranthemum A group rapidly increasing in popularity, they are sometimes called marguerites or shrubby chrysanthemums. Many have blue-tinted foliage and they come in an increasing range of flower forms: single, various anemone-centred types and doubles. Colours range from white, through a variety of pinks, to reddish tones, plus yellows and creams. Most flower from before planting out until the first sharp frost.

Of the whites, the blue-green-leaved *A. foeniculaceum*, 2 ft (60 cm), is very floriferous, 'Qinta White', 2 ft (60 cm), is a dark-leaved, anemone-centred form and 'Mrs Sanders', 2 ft (60 cm), is a shaggy double. In pink there is the single 'Gill's Pink', 2 ft (60 cm), the stunning anemone-centred 'Vancouver', 2 ft (60 cm), which fades almost to white, and the rather straggly 'Rollison's Red', 2 ft (60 cm) (see p. 127), starting red and fading to pink. In yellow there is the dwarf *A. maderense*, 18 in. (45 cm), with its rue-coloured foliage, while the floppy 'Jamaica Primrose', 2 ft (60 cm),

---

Tender perennial argyranthemums are becoming available in a wide range of cultivars. This is 'Vancouver'

Fuchsia 'Autumnale' has attractively tinted foliage

is being superseded by the more compact and very floriferous 'Yellow Star', 18 in. (45 cm).

All are best in rich conditions in sun, either in tubs or beds, and because they make substantial plants and spread well, one is enough for a large tub. Look out for aphids on overwintered plants and leaf miner on mature specimens.

Canna Another group with rather muddled names, cannas have roots like flag irises, broad foliage and flowers in various fiery shades. Most reach 4-5ft (1.2-1.5 m), and are ideal as a focal point or at the back of mixed borders. 'Yellow Humbert' has green foliage and bright yellow flowers, 'Orchid' has pink flowers and green leaves, 'Wyoming' has orange flowers and purple leaves, with 'The President' in deep red with purple leaves. Start the rhizomes into growth in 8-10 in. (20-25 cm) pots in March at 60°F (15°C), harden off and plant out after the last frost. Cannas like a rich soil, plenty of moisture and a sunny spot, and will then increase rapidly. Store the rhizomes frost-free over the winter like dahlias but do not allow them to become too dry.

Dahlia Of the many thousands of dahlias available, the dwarf bedders, 12-18 in. (30-45 cm) and those used in parks, 2-2½ ft (60-75 cm), are the most suitable, although taller cultivars can be used in larger schemes. On the whole, the small and medium cactus, waterlily and decorative forms are the most effective. It would be invidious to make recommendations when so many are available in such a wide range of shades and when most are stocked by just a few nurseries; this indicates how high the general standard is.

There are a few taller, dark-leaved dahlias which are especially worth growing, in particular 'Bishop of Llandaff', 3 ft (1 m), a glowing semi-double scarlet with almost black leaves and 'David Howard', 4 ft (1.2 m), a fully double, fiery orange with bronze foliage. Start the tubers into growth in the warmth in spring, take cuttings of 2-3 in. (5-8 cm) shoots in the propagator, pot on, harden off well before planting. Taller types will need support. Dead head regularly and beware aphids and earwigs and also red spider mite in hot dry summers.

Felicia Invaluable blue-flowered daisies for the sunniest situations, felicias are neat in growth and tougher than many tender perennials. They flower incessantly. 'Santa Anita', 12 in. (30 cm), boasts the largest flowers and also has a yellow variegated form, 'Santa Anita Variegated', 12 in. (30 cm). 'Read's White' is a useful white form but less effective than the blue. Easy to grow, green-leaved types in particular need trimming occasionally to prevent stragginess.

Fuchsia Although fewer gardeners use fuchsias in their bedding than was once the case, more are being used in baskets and window boxes and they really are very effective provided the right cultivar is chosen for the right situation. Some will even thrive on the sunless, north-facing side of a house.

There is a huge range of candidates, both of upright types for bedding and trailing types for baskets, so choose the colours that appeal. I would especially recommend those with coloured foliage, and of the upright ones I suggest *F. magellanica* 'Versicolor' with pale-edged, grey leaves and pink-flushed tips. For baskets 'Autumnale' with its coppery and rusty tints is good, as is 'Golden Swingtime', the yellow-leaved version of the well known red-and-white-flowered cultivar. Another favourite for baskets is 'Golden Marinka', with gold edged leaves and red flowers.

Most fuchsias are best in partial shade although the *triphylla* group which includes 'Thalia' are better able to stand full sun; unfortunately these require a higher winter temperature. Fuchsias appreciate good soil and steady moisture plus regular feeding for container-grown plants. They are better after overwintering as plants rather than as cuttings in pots. Check for whitefly and aphids.

Gazania Although seed-raised gazanias are improving, those

Gazania uniflora grows here in a striking combination with *Tradescantia pallida* 'Purpurea'

raised from cuttings, 12 in. (30 cm), generally have the best foliage, either variegated or silvery white, which ensures they are still attractive on those dull days when the flowers close. Of those with white and silver leaves, 'Cream Beauty' and the orange *G. uniflora* are especially good while the orange-flowered *G. rigens* 'Aureo-Variegata' has strongly yellow-edged leaves. Plant in full sun.

Geranium see **Pelargonium**

Helichrysum Mainly silver-leaved plants which are indispensable in both containers and borders. Most are vigorous with long shoots which insinuate themselves through neighbouring plants, and they look especially good with pastel colours. They can be trained as standards.

There are four main forms of *H. petiolare.* The species itself, 12-18 in. (30-45 cm), is vigorous and has heart-shaped grey leaves, 'Limelight', 12-18 in. (30-45 cm), with yellowish-green foliage is as vigorous, 'Variegatum', 12-18 in. (30-45 cm), with cream-edged leaves is a little less so, while 'Roundabout', 9 in. (23 cm), is compact and variegated. *Plecostachys serpyllifolia* is a small-leaved, bushy, rather similar grey-leaved plant formerly known as *Helichrysum microphyllum.*

An unusual combination of colours is provided by *Heliotropium*
'Chatsworth' and the rust-coloured *Calceolaria* 'Boughton'

Best in sun, partial shade also suits them but they are
surprisingly susceptible to drought, especially in containers. *H.
petiolare* is hardy in mild areas.

Heliotropium Grown for their vanilla scent as much as their
purple or lilac flowers, heliotropes are always admired when well
grown. 'Princess Marina', 18 in. (45 cm), is deep purple,
'Chatsworth', 18 in. (45 cm), is paler, 'White Lady', 12 in. (30 cm),
is a lilac-tinted white. Plant in full sun, ideal in containers on a
sheltered patio. Keep dry in winter.

Impatiens Although most impatiens (busy lizzies) are raised from
seed, New Guinea hybrids and some doubles are better from
cuttings. The foliage and flower colour of New Guinea hybrids
raised from cuttings are superior to seed-raised plants, but they
are often sold only in mixed sets or unnamed. Doubles raised from
seed will give some singles and a mixture of partial and full
doubles; cuttings-raised plants will be good doubles but again are
often sold in unnamed mixtures. Best as container plants, grow in
sheltered conditions and keep moist. Overwinter as plants rather
than cuttings and beware red spider mite both outdoors and in the
greenhouse.

Shrubby *Lantana camara* can be trained as a standard plant to grow in a container or form a centrepiece for a bedding scheme

Lantana Unfashionable but delightful plants with a spreading habit and clusters of bright flowers in reds, pinks, yellows, oranges and white but often sold simply by colour rather than by name. Best in full sun, plagued by whitefly in most seasons, so regular treatment will probably be necessary. Rather fragile.

Lotus Delightful, ferny, silver-leaved trailers with parrot's-beak flowers, their spring flowering season means that in summer they are mainly used as foliage plants. *L. berthelotii* has brilliant red flowers in spring on the previous year's growth, 'Kew Form' also flowers in autumn. Full sun and constant moisture encourages the best foliage, drought will cause the needle-like leaves to drop. Overwinter as plants for flowers in the greenhouse in spring.

Osteospermums, like argyranthemums, are becoming very popular with many new cultivars to choose from. This is 'Buttermilk'

Osteospermum Sometimes known as dimorphothecas, osteospermums have daisy flowers in a wide range of colours. They vary in habit and fall into two main groups, the stiffly upright and the flat and ground-hugging, the latter being almost hardy.

'Buttermilk', 2 ft (60 cm), is creamy yellow, 'Whirligig', 2 ft (60 cm), is blue and white with spoon-shaped petals and has a pink version, 'Pink Whirls'; these are upright types. Low-growing 'Cannington Roy', 6 in. (15 cm), is pinkish purple with a white eye, and *O. ecklonis* 'Prostratum', 6 in. (15 cm), is white with a blue eye. There are two upright variegated osteospermums, 'Silver Sparkler', 2 ft (60 cm), with white flowers and white-edged leaves and 'Bodegas Pink', 2 ft (60 cm), with pink flowers and cream-edged leaves.

Osteospermums are best in full sun, with good soil. They are easy to root and overwinter well, but rooted cuttings may continue to grow in even the coolest winter conditions and so need potting up early.

Pelargonium Most zonal and ivy-leaved pelargoniums can be grown outside in the summer months, although the fully double types suffer badly from botrytis. With so many to choose from specific recommendations are unnecessary, but of the zonals the Irenes and the singles with the Highfield prefix are reliable groups, as are the woodier Uniques. All the ivy-leaved types thrive outside but the Cascade series of continental pelargoniums is especially floriferous. Plant them in full sun and although they are drought tolerant they are more prolific, flower longer and keep their foliage better if kept moist but not soggy. They are best overwintered as young plants.

Salvia Most salvias for bedding are raised from seed but better plants of *S. patens*, 18 in. (45 cm), are raised by overwintering. This is an elegant plant with relatively few flowers compared with

Pelargoniums are among the most popular bedding plants, much used in hanging baskets and containers. This is 'Salmon Unique'

seed-raised salvia, but they are much bigger and hooked in shape. The species is rich gentian blue in colour, 'Cambridge Blue' is pale blue, 'Chilcombe' is misty lilac and there is a rare white. This species has tuberous roots and can be overwintered like a dahlia. The best plants are grown by simply replanting the whole root, but cuttings can be taken of the new growth in spring and these will make better plants than seedlings.

Verbena Unlike most seed-raised annual verbenas, those grown as tender perennials are generally spreading in habit and make fine basket and tub plants as well as covering the ground well in borders. There are two groups, dark green with cut leaves and paler green with lobed leaves.

Verbenas are sometimes sold simply by colour which may be red, various purples, lilacs, and pinks plus white and one or two bicolours. 'Lawrence Johnston', 12 in. (30 cm), is a brilliant red, 'Silver Anne', 12 in. (30 cm), a soft pink which is almost hardy, 'Sissinghurst', 9 in. (23 cm), is a cut-leaved cerisey pink, 'Loveliness', 12 in. (30 cm), is deep lilac, 'Carousel', 9 in. (23 cm), is a cut-leaved purple striped with white and 'White Knight', 12 in. (30 cm), is pure white. Full sun suits them best and they are among the easiest of all to grow; some will overwinter outside in mild seasons. Cuttings root very easily, even of old wood, and they usually layer themselves, too.

Other summer bedders from cuttings There are many more tender perennials used as summer bedders, everything from bananas to palms, but there are a few others that you are more likely to come across. The white variegated spider plant, **_Chlorophytum elatum_** **'Vittatum'** makes a wonderful bedder but is best planted out as a good-sized plant. The blue-flowered **_Convolvulus sabatius_** with its small, bindweed-like flowers and trailing habit is good in containers, while **_Glechoma hederacea_** **'Variegata'** with its small, white-edged foliage trails so determinedly that it simply falls vertically down over the edge of the basket. One cuttings-raised lobelia is worth growing, the semi-trailing **_Lobelia richardii_** with its large pale blue, white-eyed flowers and bronze-tinted foliage. The stiff arching growth of **_Plectranthus coleoides_** **'Variegatus'** is very distinctive and very showy in tubs with its white-edged leaves; and **Scaevola**, with flowers like those of perennial lobelias in blue and purple on long trailing shoots, are also fine container plants. Finally, another variegated plant, **_Sedum lineare_** **'Variegatum'**, with its pale green leaves edged with cream, is proving another good foliage plant for baskets.

—— Ideas for Summer Bedding ——

Summer bedding plants are very adaptable. They come in a wide range of colours, flower forms and sizes, so whatever you need for a planned display can be found in the catalogues. It is true that few thrive in full shade but in partial shade and full sun the range is staggering, and choosing superb plants for the traditional combination of red salvia, blue lobelia and white alyssum is as easy as getting away from it altogether and trying something quite different.

BEDDING SCHEMES

Formal bedding schemes provoke strong opinions – some people love them, others will not have them in the garden and even dislike them in parks. But in the right situation, especially in formal gardens, they can be very successful, and in these days of interest in unusual plants a formal bedding scheme featuring an imaginative combination of colourful but slightly unexpected plants can be very successful.

The parks approach, which infiltrated private gardens long ago, was to use a low edging surrounding a slightly taller carpet with dot plants for emphasis; plants raised from seed and from cuttings were mixed. A modern example might feature an edging of bronze-leaved *Lobelia* 'Crystal Palace' with a main planting of *Tagetes* 'Solar Sulphur' Afro-French marigolds with, in a large bed, a clump of *Ricinus communis* 'Impala' added. Segmented circles were also popular and in recent years plantings with curved outlines within a rectangular bed are being used more. Showing off one variety entirely on its own, especially a mixture like *Pelargonium* Sensation or *Impatiens* Super Elfin Pastel, perhaps with silver foliage, can be stunning.

Informal plantings are often more suitable, with beds of a less regular outline planted in less regimental fashion. In fact, the same rules that apply to planting a herbaceous or mixed border can apply to bedding except that you can rely on most summer

Aptly called Tapestry, this mixture of *Nemesia* (see p.91) would look pretty in a bed on its own

bedders to flower all summer, so you can largely forget the problem of flowering time.

Perhaps this is the time to sound a warning about mixtures. Most bedders are available in mixtures and are very popular, but they must be used carefully. Planting mixtures of different plants alongside each other is usually a recipe for disastrous clashes; they are best used alone or separated from other mixtures by foliage plants or single colours. But in the same way that planting five different colours of Michaelmas daisy in one clump in a herbaceous border would rarely be successful, mixtures of bedding plants can also disappoint. My advice is always to give them a bed or a corner of their own.

Arranging a bedding scheme like a herbaceous border gives an appropriately informal look. Plants are set in groups of varying informal shapes and although the tallest should generally go at the back of the bed or the centre of island beds, and the planting then grade down to the smallest at the front, this must be a variable rule. Bedding plants are also much more flamboyant than perennials, so you may have to consider using more foliage plants or flowering plants with valuable foliage than you would otherwise – the effect might be just too shocking. Thus coloured-leaved fuchsias, some of the more delicately coloured pelargoniums including scented-leaved types, cannas, abutilons, silver-leaved cinerarias and artemesias can all be invaluable in maintaining a calm tone.

BEDDING WITH PERMANENT PLANTINGS

Leaving spaces in mixed borders for groups of bedding plants allows you an element of change in an otherwise relatively permanent planting. Each summer and spring you can add welcome variation to your borders. Many gardeners are worried by the fact that some bedding plants look out of place in mixed or herbaceous borders. So the plants you choose must not only be of a colour appropriate to nearby shrubs or perennials but must also have a habit and bearing that fit in – otherwise the effect will make you cringe. Fortunately it is usually possible to find exactly the right plant. For example, you may be looking for a fiery orange flower to go at the front of a border alongside the perennial *Heuchera* 'Palace Purple'; a dwarf African marigold might look ridiculous while *Sanvitalia procumbens* would be ideal and could be followed by a dainty viola for spring.

CONTAINERS

Plants specially intended for tubs and hanging baskets are appearing more frequently in garden centres and catalogues. Although the more compact bedders are suitable, plants with a trailing habit are useful to tumble cheerfully over the edge. Plants which tolerate root competition, limited soil space, and the possibility of drying out are invaluable. Watering is usually the problem; if you can rely on containers never being neglected for a scorching weekend, then use mimulus and impatiens; if not, stick to pelargoniums and cineraria. Purpose-made container composts with extra water-holding capacity help the plants withstand drought but watering must be frequent and generous in late summer when temperatures are high and water loss is at its greatest, while roots fill the container and extract moisture at a rapid rate.

Foliage is invaluable in containers as it knits plantings together both in a physical way and by creating allies of neighbouring colours. The silver-leaved *Plecostachys serpyllifolia* will link together pink *Argyranthemum* 'Vancouver', *Lobelia* 'Light Blue Fountain' and perhaps a white multiflora petunia to make a lovely picture.

A colourful combination of argyranthemums, lobelia, fuchsia and bidens

Spring Plants

Compared with the vast array of flowers available for summer from both seed and cuttings, the selection for spring is relatively sparse. Fortunately it does include two groups, pansies and primulas, which provide an exceptionally full range of colours. There is also more scope than in summer for using bulbs with the bedding plants to create a more varied display.

SPRING BEDDING FROM SEED

Almost all spring bedding plants are raised from seed and there are two main methods. Traditionally most were raised entirely out of doors, starting off by sowing the seed in a seed bed in summer. In recent years more plants have been raised under glass and this is partly a response to the increasing cost of F_1 hybrid seed and the relatively small number of seeds supplied in a packet.

RAISING OUT OF DOORS

Virtually no facilities or equipment are required for raising seed out of doors, but the soil should be rich, reasonably well drained and ideally shaded for about half the day; a part of the vegetable plot is often ideal. Plants suitable for raising outside include wallflowers, sweet williams, daisies, forget-me-nots, honesty and the cheaper pansies.

Seed is sown thinly in rows in June or July, just as you would sow hardy annuals or vegetables. If the soil is dry, it pays to water the individual rows from the spout of the watering can immediately before sowing the seed. After germination, the seedlings are thinned carefully, first to 1 in. (2.5 cm) apart, then thinned again, the distance depending on the plant and the cultivar. Place a finger on either side of each seedling to be retained so that it is not disturbed when its neighbour is removed.

The next stage depends largely on the plant concerned, how many seedlings you have and how many you need. Wallflowers

Wall pots filled with pansies and trailing ivy, a simple and pleasing arrangement for winter and spring

and sweet williams are best transplanted 6-9 in. (15-23 cm) apart to give them plenty of space to grow on; pansies and daisies can simply be thinned to 4-6 in. (10-15 cm) apart although if you need every seedling these, too, can be transplanted. They will need a thorough watering after thinning or transplanting and will also appreciate a little more sun at this stage. Protect them from slugs and aphids.

RAISING INDOORS

Some seed is too expensive to risk in the open ground and is best raised in a greenhouse or cold frame; this applies especially to pansies, polyanthus and primroses. These are sown in pots in the same way as summer bedding and then stood under the bench in a cold greenhouse or outside in a shaded frame to germinate. Standard peat, coco-fibre or loam-based composts are all suitable but all-peat composts may need additional drainage. They should be pricked out into trays at 35 seedlings to a standard tray, again using a standard compost, then for the best-quality plants they should be moved on individually into 3½ in. (9 cm) pots. If you only need a small number of plants of each variety you could prick them out directly into pots. Propagation trays divided into cells are also useful here. After pricking out they should be grown on in a shady frame. Do not keep them in the warmth of the greenhouse as growth will be leggy.

If you have no greenhouse or frame but still wish to give expensive seed the care it deserves, then sow in pots, stand the pots in a deep box in a shady corner and cover it with shade netting or sacking to keep the seed cool and exclude birds and mice. Prick out into trays and stand them in a cool, partially shaded spot or one shaded from the side rather than overhead. Stand the trays on stones to keep out worms and protect them from slugs.

PLANTING OUT

Plants grown in the open ground should be planted in the autumn, generally about the end of September when the summer bedding is finished, but the exact timing will vary from season to season. Lift the plants carefully, keeping as much soil as possible on the roots. Place them in a box and cover the roots in soil to protect against drying out until replanted. Plant firmly in their flowering place and water in well. Plants raised in trays are generally best

White double daisies, *Bellis perennis*, and wallflowers make an attractive display for a raised, round bed

planted in the autumn, too, so that they have a little time before the winter to settle down. When planting a bed or container with a mixture of bedders and spring bulbs, it is usually impractical to plant the bulbs in the autumn and the bedders in spring. Plant the bedders in autumn and set the bulbs amongst them immediately afterwards.

Pot-grown plants can be planted in the autumn or can be kept through the winter in a cold frame. They should not be over-protected, but covered only in periods of hard frost, gales or downpours. If the plants are cosseted they will grow soft and be easily damaged when they are finally planted out in spring.

Most spring bedders, including pansies and primulas, are best in a rich soil that is not too wet and in full sun; most will also tolerate partial shade but full overhead shade is a less successful situation unless the trees casting the shade come into leaf late. The compost for containers needs to be well drained, especially if planted in the autumn.

Ideas for Spring Bedding

In general, spring bedding plants are suited to a wider range of situations than summer plants. They are less gaudy, less dumpy in their habit and so fit in much better with other spring plants. Like summer plants, their uses can be divided into bedding schemes, plantings in permanent borders and containers.

As well as the traditional bedding scheme of a dwarf edging surrounding a taller carpet and the mixing of wallflowers and bulbs, many spring plants look good as plantings of single colours or mixtures, and in less formal plantings in formal beds. Wallflower 'Primrose Bedder' is lovely edged with pansy 'Joker' or forget-me-not 'Marine'. 'Blood Red' wallflowers can be interplanted with 'White Triumphator' lily-flowered tulips for example, and wallflower 'Harlequin' and pansy 'Ultima' make especially attractive mixed plantings. Sweet williams, being later flowering than most spring plants, are best treated separately.

Most spring plants fit well into mixed borders; only some of the more garish pansies and polyanthus are best kept to themselves. Unfortunately there are no spring plants of a height sufficient to make an impact at the back of the border except foxgloves, but with so few other plants to obscure the view in April and May, plants such as honesty, sweet williams and taller wallflowers can still be very effective.

Tubs, window boxes and hanging baskets, especially in sunny and sheltered spots, are ideal sites for spring plants, for that slight protection will encourage strong growth and early flowering. It pays to keep spring schemes simple – just one variety of pansy, for example, or pink daisies with blue grape hyacinths. Containers provide the ideal site for some of the many pansies in unusual shades which have appeared in recent years, and for primroses and polyanthus in more interesting colours. Many of the primroses in seed catalogues are not hardy enough for the open garden, so have a better chance in a sheltered container.

Red and yellow tulips interplanted with wallflowers in matching colours, and blue forget-me-nots

A to Z of Plants
for Spring Bedding

Although there are far fewer spring plants available in catalogues, in some subjects there is an astonishing variety.

Bellis Double daisies come with either neat pompons or larger, shaggier flowers. The colours are restricted to reds, pinks and white. Spring Star, 4-6 in. (10-15 cm), is a large-flowered, pompon mix which includes an unusual blood-red shade; Pomponette, 4-6 in. (10-15 cm), has smaller pompon flowers in three shades while Goliath, 6-8 in. (15-20 cm), has shaggy flowers up to 3 in. (8 cm) across. Best sown in the open and transplanted, these daisies are lovely window box plants, and good edging for small beds.

Forget-me-not (*Myosotis*) This spring favourite is easy to raise and its airy habit makes it an ideal contrast with other plants. There are tall and some rather dumpy forms. 'Marine', 6 in. (15 cm), is deep blue, 'Ultramarine', 10 in. (25 cm), is the best all round variety, while 'Blue Bouquet', 15 in. (38 cm), is good in larger borders. There are also those with pink and white flowers but these are generally less successful. Raise in the open ground or in boxes; in dry seasons their display may be curtailed by mildew.

Foxglove (*Digitalis*) Foxgloves may last for several years but flower best in the second year and move well in autumn. Excelsior, 5 ft (1.5 m), is a wonderful tall mixture, Foxy, 3 ft (1 m), is more compact. Both have flowers all around the stem. For bedding, raise outside and transplant with plenty of soil on the roots.

Honesty (*Lunaria annua*) Biennials which are often left to self-sow, they make impressive bedders and being taller than wallflowers are especially valuable. 'Munstead Purple', 3 ft (1 m), is rich purple while 'Alba', 3 ft (1 m), is pure white. Raise outside, taking especial care to keep the soil on the roots when transplanting.

Pansy and viola (*Viola*) The most popular spring bedders, now available in an astonishing range of colours. Some are known as winter-flowering and will flower in the autumn, in mild spells in winter and swing into their stride early in spring; others are more genuinely spring flowering. Violas are smaller flowered, more dainty and spring flowering.

The best winter-flowering mixture is Ultima in 27 shades although Universal is still popular; Ultima Pastel Mix includes only the pale shades and is very pretty. Many of the colours in the Ultima and Universal mixtures are available separately. Of the spring pansies Turbo and Majestic Giants are good while Spring Ovation is a more economical mix. 'Jolly Joker' is a cheeky blue and white, 'Delft' is cream and blue, 'Padparadja' is orange and Love Duet is cream or white with a raspberry blotch. The catalogues list many other delightful and unusual colours. In violas Bambini is a gold eyed mixture while Princess is a lovely mixture of blue, yellow, cream and a purple/white bicolour.

Sow indoors and grow on in trays or pots. Keep cool and on the dry side, planting out in winter or spring. Ideal for bedding and especially good in window boxes and in hanging baskets.

Polyanthus (*Primula*) An old favourite for spring, there are those with large flowers and bright colours as well as ones in more subtle and unusual shades. Some have been developed as pot plants and may perform poorly in the open garden.

Crescendo, 9 in. (23 cm), is a large-flowered mixture in seven yellow-eyed shades, Rainbow, 9 in. (23 cm), in eight eyed shades has smaller flowers but more of them and is usually more effective. These can be planted in the autumn with confidence. The Pacific Giants, 12 in. (30 cm), are less hardy and are best set out in spring. The Barnhaven series, 9 in. (23 cm), come in some wonderful pastel shades and rich eyeless colours, are perfectly hardy but are now difficult to obtain.

Polyanthus are best raised in a cold greenhouse or frame but should be kept cool as high temperatures can inhibit germination. Ensure the seed compost is well drained, do not cover the seed with compost but keep humid with glass or clingfilm. Sieve a little compost over the seed as soon as it has germinated to anchor the seedlings.

Primrose (*Primula*) Most primroses in the catalogues are intended to be grown as pot plants and although some may be grown successfully in containers in sheltered spots, few thrive in the open garden. As well as the usual bright colours, there are dainty bicolours and those with dark leaves.

The pick of the bedding primroses are undoubtedly the Wanda Hybrids, 4-6 in. (10-15 cm), which are vigorous, very hardy and come in a range of seven colours, all with rich green or bronze-tinted leaves. Husky, 6 in. (15 cm), is a good, brightly coloured,

The Wanda Hybrids have attractive foliage and flowers in a range of subtle, old-fashioned colours

green-leaved mix. The Juliana Hybrids, 4-6 in. (10-15 cm), in a wide range of dainty bicolours, are a little less tough. Raise them in the same way as polyanthus.

Stocks (*Matthiola*) Wonderfully scented plants in delightful soft shades, ideal for patio containers. Two types feature as spring bedders, Brompton stocks and East Lothian stocks. Brompton stocks reach about 18 in. (45 cm), and can be selected for doubleness and flower in May and June. East Lothian stocks reach 9-12 in. (23-30 cm), flower in June and July, but are not selectable for doubles.

Selectable Mixed is the only Brompton mixture which is selectable for doubleness; the doubles have light green leaves and these should be grown on for the best plants. Legacy is the best East Lothian type and you should expect 80 per cent doubles. The colours in both mixtures are shades of red, pink, purple, lilac and white.

Massed Brompton stocks with an edging of ivy

Both types are best sown in the greenhouse in June or July and pricked out into 3½ in. (9 cm) pots for overwintering in a cold frame before planting out in mid March. Watch for grey mould on the plants during the winter.

Sweet william (*Dianthus*) Of all the dianthus only sweet william are treated as spring bedders. They flower later than most, which means they do not combine well with other spring plants, and they also disrupt the planting of the summer bedding. Auricula Eyed, 18 in. (45 cm), comes in red and pink shades, each with a white eye, Monarch, 18 in. (45 cm), in rich and pastel shades, while Indian Carpet, 9-12 in. (23-30 cm), is a good dwarfer mixture; 'Crimson Velvet', 18 in. (45 cm), is a fine blood-red shade. Sow outside and transplant with plenty of soil on the roots. When grown for cutting, the plants can be left in place for a second year.

Viola see **Pansy**

Wallflowers (*Cheiranthus* and *Erysimum*) Wallflowers are much better raised at home than bought from markets or garden centres where they are usually stood in buckets of water for days while the roots rot; they are very easy and you will be able to grow the separate colours rarely found on sale as plants. They come in three types, taller ones at about 18 in. (45 cm), dwarf ones at 10-12 in.

(25-30 cm), and Siberian wallflowers, 9 in. (23 cm), which are a little later flowering and mound forming rather than upright and bushy.

Of the taller ones, Harlequin is a fine mixture and there are some lovely separate colours such as 'Blood Red', the orangey-red 'Fire King', 'Purple Gem' and the bright yellow 'Cloth of Gold'. Bedder is the best of the shorter growing mixtures with separate colours available in gold, orange, primrose and scarlet. Pastel Shades, 12 in. (30 cm), includes many unusual colours not found in most mixtures. 'Orange Bedder' is a brilliant orange Siberian type.

Sow outside from May to July; leave it late in windy areas or your plants will be too big to remain stable after planting out. Wallflowers are susceptible to clubroot so incorporate them into the brassica rotation on the vegetable plot. Do not try to raise them in pots.

'Little Darling' (see p.86) has unusual open-throated flowers. Like other antirrhinums it may suffer from rust

Pests and Diseases

Early in the life of spring and summer bedding plants, disease can be prevented by using clean pots and trays, fresh composts (never garden soil) and water direct from the mains, not from a water butt. Preventative treatment with a copper fungicide also helps. Once through the early stages, there is generally no need to spray but checks should be made regularly and any problem dealt with promptly to prevent its spread. Good hygiene, careful watering and drenching with a copper fungicide will help prevent damping off, when seedlings collapse in the pots or trays, and blackleg. Good air flow in frames and greenhouses and regular removal of dead leaves and flowers will help prevent botrytis, but carbendazim spray will cure it. Aphids can be a problem; the specific aphid killer pirimicarb harms few other insects. Powdery mildew can be very destructive in hot seasons on verbenas and violas; propiconazole will deal with it effectively and with rust on antirrhinums. Derris will kill or at least restrict red spider mite and is good against small caterpillars.

Matricaria 'Snow Dwarf' used as an edging plant for a bed of *Argyranthemum* 'Rollison's Red' (see p.103)

Fragrant and Aromatic Plants

—— KAY N. SANECKI ——

Roses and lavender bring fragrance to the garden. Here blocks of dark *Lavandula angustifolia* 'Munstead' alternate with paler L. *angustifolia* 'Loddon Pink'

Roses and lavender look good together and smell delicious

plants in tubs or boxes that can be moved from place to place. Window boxes also bring scent to where it can be enjoyed, especially by the housebound. Another idea is to plant against a warm wall where the radiated heat from the brickwork or stonework will enhance evening scent and help to lengthen the period of enjoyment. It is a remarkable fact that the supply of essential oils, and therefore scent, from a plant seems to be inexhaustible, and is often related to the weather, warmth encouraging more scent. Pathways can be dotted with aromatic plants that tolerate being trodden on, or lined with sub-shrubs that when brushed in passing donate their contribution to the enjoyment of the garden.

Holding aloft is the major way in which scented plants can be enjoyed. Space in the garden may not allow for a pergola, but simple canopies like car ports, or patio arbours, can support scented climbers. Trellis formed of, or covered by, 'Netlon'-style mesh can form bays in borders, nose-high fences, screens, arches or columns to support various scent-producing plants. A simple tripod or 'wigwam' of canes, strategically placed, can be a decorative feature and at the same time allow air to pick up the scent. Old tree stumps, dilapidated sheds and disused seats all offer support for fragrant scramblers to good garden effect.

Consider the evening-scented qualities of plants in gardens where the owners are away at work during the day, or use the prevailing breeze to waft a scent towards the windows of the house or to the patio. The season of flowering or garden effect obviously has to be taken into consideration as with any other garden planning, and while care needs to be exercised in not masking a delicate scent by an overpowering one, in practice it hardly ever happens that scents clash and become unacceptable.

Catmint, *Nepeta* × *faassenii*, makes a good edging plant for paths (see p. 143)

Herbaceous Perennials and Annuals

In the decorative garden it is the flowering plants that provide the blocks of colour, varying from one month to the next. Relatively few of them are richly scented although these are the ones we gather to form a true nosegay. Many of them are hardy perennials and because they are raised and managed easily they are popular, and are often the first plants the amateur attempts to grow. Flowering plants are usually grouped for colour effect and form in borders, or on the edge of shrub borders; nowhere do they look better than when massed among others of their kind. The contrast of one colour or leaf form, or even plant form, with the next is part of garden artistry.

In the border, the year starts with the bergenias, or elephant ears, so sweetly scented, the more so when taken indoors, and soon after come the erysimums, closely related to the wallflower. Then follow irises and peonies, *Crambe cordifolia* for the back of the border or a rough area, achilleas and their relative, tansy. Fragrant annuals to try include *Lobularia maritima*, available with flowers in rich pinks as well as white, nasturtium (*Tropaeolum majus*), marigold (*Calendula officinalis*, see p. 136), French and African marigolds (*Tagetes*) and the sweetest scented of all, the sweet pea (*Lathyrus odoratus*). Present-day dwarf varieties of sweet pea are deliciously scented and at the same time they are labour-saving and can be used to good effect as border edges or to line a path where the fragrance can be enjoyed.

The tree lupin (*Lupinus arboreus*) is easily raised from seed and lingers for a few years in many areas, forming a shrubby base and sprouting fragrant yellow flowers. It is soon established and therefore useful for quick effect in a new garden.

Cheiranthus cheiri, the wallflower, is normally cultivated as a biennial; seed is sown one spring to flower in the following year (see p. 136). Few plants are as hardy and tolerant of any and every situation, be it open border, or container, and utterly reliable for a good spring show. Their perfume is among the richest of all flower perfumes, riding on the air even from one garden to the next, when

---

Heliotropium arborescens (*H. peruvianum*), cherry pie, is an almond-scented half hardy annual (see p. 140)

Above: Wallflowers, *Cheiranthus cheiri*
Below: Pot marigold, *Calendula officinalis*

planted in a mass. Single or double velvety flowers come in a wide range of colour from cream to deep maroon and brilliant orange, crimson and purple. Best results are achieved when seed is sown early in spring and plants transplanted to permanent quarters in late September or October. Sun or semi-shade seem to make little difference to the results, but they respond to good conditions. Do not feed after planting.

***Convallaria majalis*, lily-of-the-valley,** (see p. 139), produces a scent sweeter than any other plant. Native of our woodlands and therefore thriving best in leafmouldy, moist situations, it has dainty clear white rounded bells dangling along one side of the stiff stem. The foliage pierces the ground first like a little rolled umbrella before opening into twin broad flat leaves in early May. Choose shade or semi-shade beneath trees or shrubs or in woodland or on a north-facing bank for the most satisfactory results, and heed a predeliction for chalky soil. The perfume persists, even after cutting, until the flowers fade. Specially prepared crowns are available for gentle forcing in pots, when the flowers will bloom in the conservatory or porch in March and April.

***Dianthus*, carnations and pinks or gillyflowers** Among the oldest of cultivated plants, there is no doubt that they have been cherished for their delicious fragrance. Always spicy and full bodied, some scents display distinct clove-like overtones – lending the name, for example, to 'clove pink'. They flourish on chalk and almost bare limestone to produce dainty flat-faced little flowers held at right angles to the stem and set off by a tuft of grey-green thick grass-like leaves. Various sorts are useful for the rock garden, tucked into wall pockets, for pots, troughs or open border or as conservatory decoration. Most can be grown from seed, and there is an almost bewildering choice of named cultivars, all of which carry the distinctive scent. Some are annual, many perennial, and the latter can be propagated from cuttings or layers or by division after flowering.

***Dianthus barbatus*, sweet william,** (see p. 139), stand apart from the remainder of the dianthus in that the flowers are held together in a broad flattened head, fringed by a green beard. They are proudly upstanding on tough bright green stems and offer a rich perfume, sweeter and less clove-toned than their relatives, the pinks. Generally, the auricula-eyed forms bear the sweetest scent. Sweet william is a short-lived perennial, and is often grown as a biennial, especially in the colder areas; cutting back after flowering will encourage the basal growth to thicken up and make a bolder plant and at the same time prolong life.

Dianthus caryophyllus is the species from which the hardy border carnations have been developed. Border carnations are short-lived perennials and not at their best in the mixed flower border. They have double frilled flowers often with notched petals and a rather nutmeg-clove scent deeper than that of the pinks, and bloom mainly in July and August. A strain intermediate between the border carnation and the perpetual-flowering (glasshouse) carnation is known as 'cottage' carnations. They have shorter stouter stems and the flowering season extends to September. Seedsmen's lists are worth perusing and novelties are worth trying, especially as an experiment to grow in a pot.

Dianthus plumaris, the pink, no longer lives up to this name but comes in the most glorious colour range – especially among the hybrid allwoodii sorts. Hardy, pert, tolerant of drought, lime and clipping, pinks will flower over a long period from their peak in midsummer until well into September. Their faces are painted or plain and they are generally grouped according to the way in which the colour is disposed on the petals; self (one colour), bi-color, laced or fancy. The classification depends upon parentage, and as scent is transferred from parents to progeny, all groups have a place in the fragrant garden. The groups are garden pinks, allwoodii pinks, London pinks, and hybrid alpine pinks.

Garden pinks are mainly heavily scented and burst into flower once only during June. Burst is perhaps the most appropriate word because they all suffer from an inadequate calyx which splits, allowing the petals to spill out of formation. The well-known 'Mrs Sinkins' is an example.

Allwoodii pinks are distinctly clove-scented, with a neater habit, somewhat squat. Invaluable as border edging plants, they flower intermittently between June and August. Most bear Christian names, easily remembered when identified with one's acquaintances: 'Doris', 'Isobel', Monty' and 'Ian'.

London pinks are really a cross between the two previous groups (with some other intermarrying too) and have pretty flowers laced and edged with deeper colours usually matching the eye. Quite long in the stem for pinks, but not too lanky to be useful border plants, they are so-called because their names commemorate the capital: 'London Lovely' and 'London Poppet'.

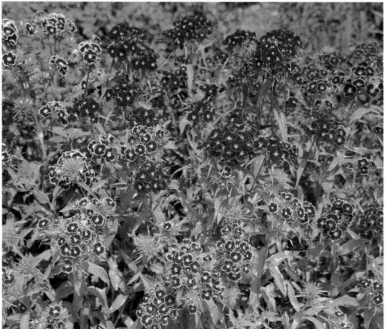

Above: Lily-of-the-valley, *Convallaria majalis*, has one of the most favoured scents (see p. 137).
Below: *Dianthus barbatus*, sweet william (see p. 137)

Hybrid alpine pinks are those small plants that are perfect for a trough on the patio, or for growing among paving or in walls. Their small flowers bloom over a long period in June and July, scenting the air for all they are worth. The real alpine pinks originate from *D. alpinus* and are diminutive plants, smothered in tiny flowers throughout the spring and summer and they are useful for the rock garden. Crosses have been made with them and *D.* × *allwoodii* and a packet of seed of Allwoodii Alpinus Mixed could produce a host of variations on the theme of little pink fringed faces with eye colours from the lipstick range.

Filipendula ulmaria, the meadowsweet or queen of the meadows, used to be known as *Spiraea ulmaria*, and is still occasionally catalogued thus. Enjoy it for its deep, over-sweet almond fragrance, sometimes a little fishy during very dry weather. Frothy creamy white blossoms, held upright on good stems decorated with fern-like leaves, look particularly good at the margin of a pond or in damp areas. It prefers damp soils and will thrive in full sun or semi-shade. Track it down in its decorative-leaved forms of 'Aurea' or 'Variegata' to add an air of gaiety to the garden when it is in flower during July and August.

Heliotropium arborescens (H. peruvianum), cherry pie, grown for its almost sickly almond scent, is best cultivated as a half hardy annual (see p. 134). Use it as a border to flower beds, as an edging to a path or in tubs and give it good drainage, for it hates to have wet roots. Pot up a few seedlings to grow in the conservatory or porch, where they will flower long after their companions used for summer bedding have been cleared. The leaves are an interesting deep green and many-veined and form a good backing to the clustered deep purple and white flowers. Various flower colours have been selected and are available from seedsmen; those paler in colour seem to be stronger in fragrance.

Hesperis matronalis, sweet rocket or dame's violet, is one of the loveliest of cottage garden plants for dry limy soil. It is a biennial that once grown will seed itself about the garden and stay for many years to produce lilac and purple or sometimes white flowerheads on tall swaying stems in May. Double-flowered forms are worth seeking out and are considered to be more strongly scented. During the day its violet fragrance needs to be sought out but twilight strengthens it to a rich sweet scent with spicy overtones that spill out on to the surrounding air. A lovely evening garden plant which

Limnanthes douglasii, the poached egg plant

our ancestors used to call queen's gillyflower, because it was considered superior in scent to all the other gillyflowers, that is, stocks, wallflowers and pinks.

***Limnanthes douglasii,* poached egg plant,** because the white daisy-like flowers are marked with a broad shiny yellow central disc. But that is the only resemblance to eggs; the scent is rich and sweet, especially in calm weather. Used as a border edging plant, scattered among paving stones or used to cover a bank, limnanthes produces a lovely effect of flowing foam. It will flower from May until late summer, attracting bees to the garden. Perfectly hardy in spite of being a Californian native, it will spread in areas where seed has been sown and stay for several years by re-seeding itself.

***Melilotus officinalis,* yellow melilot,** is probably shunned by the purists as a wild plant and weed, but it is a good nectar plant, producing lovely branches of sweet-smelling golden pea-like flowers at midsummer. Formerly a fodder plant and now creeping into herb gardens, it is worth a corner where the soil may be poor and the sun can light up its yellow flowers for at least half the day. Dry the sprigs to enjoy the fragrance as it increases and lasts. It is a biennial, and seed is available from seedsmen specialising in wild flowers. It is also a good bee plant.

***Monarda didyma,* bergamot or bee balm,** is a quick-growing perennial, which loves nothing better than a good supply of moisture-retentive material about its roots. Good clumps are formed, often deteriorating in the middle after three years or so; therefore constant division is the key to continued success. Flowers of the species are a deep glowing red arranged in whorls around the stem and there are cultivars with various coloured flowers, all retaining the scent: 'Croftway Pink', 'Snow Maiden', 'Prairie Night' and 'Hartswood Wine'. But the most popular is 'Cambridge Scarlet' which is a good red. The foliage holds much of the perfume, but the whole plant is impregnated and, even after top growth is cut back in winter, the roots safeguard the orange-like scent. A delightful plant to dry and mix into *pot pourri*; or add both fresh flowers and leaves to a summer salad or fruit cup to delight your friends.

Monarda didyma, bergamot or bee balm

Nepeta × faassenii, catmint, has aromatic leaves

Nepeta, catmints, revel in the sunshine but appreciate a good loam about their roots, where the drainage must be good. They are perfect nosegay plants, with dainty blue flowers and grey-green strongly aromatic leaves. The whole plant is richly endowed with a minty aroma – even the stems – which is retained after flowering, though in a more musty range. A brush of the hand in passing is sufficient to persuade nepetas to give away their perfume.

Nepeta cataria, catnip, is a native British plant of the hedgerows and good garden forms are available as seed from specialist seedsmen. A dainty plant with tiny white flowers, its mint-like leaves smell strongly of mint and pennyroyal. It is a rather straggly plant, and one to tuck among others. In May and June a few fresh or dried leaves infused constitute the catnip tea of former times.

Nepeta × faassenii is the catmint that forms soft decorative hummocks of deep lavender blue flower spikes and soft grey foliage in May and June (see p. 133 and above). Ensure good drainage for it, especially in winter, and choose a sunny position. Plant several to form a path edge or use them to decorate the side of steps. Invaluable used as a dry wall plant or in raised beds or on banks where it can be allowed to spread as ground cover. Propagate from cuttings or divide in autumn or spring. Use the flower spikes and

A border of mixed *Nicotiana alata*, the tobacco plant

foliage in *pot pourri*. A fine tall-growing garden hybrid 'Six Hills' is not as readily available as it used to be.

Nicotiana Tobacco plants are often hispid (bristly) and tacky to the touch and produce a distinctive fragrance from their tubular flowers with flat starry mouths. Give them shelter from prevailing winds and plant in groups for the best effect. Put them near a patio or evening sitting-out corner because the rich fragrance is then at its best. They like a deep rich moist soil.

Nicotiana alata (often catalogued as *N. affinis*) is best treated as a half hardy annual and used in raised beds or tubs near the house. Although it is a bit languid during the day, the flowering tobacco comes to life in the evening, flinging wonderful scent to the wind. Modern hybrids stay awake much of the day, and their perfume is richer in the evening. The white and purple-flowered ones are strongest in fragrance, the green ones are scentless; the oranges and yellow are intermediate. With such improvements in flower power, some of the nicotianas are useful as bedding plants and for growing in tubs; they also flourish in pots to scent the conservatory. Many half hardy annuals sown in autumn will provide early spring flowers and nicotianas are no exception though they will be killed by frost.

144

Nicotiana sylvestris is one of the most dramatic tobacco plants, given a good sheltered border or grown in a tub or large pot. Treat it as a half hardy annual. It is a somewhat coarse plant but produces long trumpet-like white flowers in midsummer that burst and dangle from the top of the stem and give off a truly wonderful fragrance in the evening. Plant it in tubs on the patio or near a porch where the scent can be enjoyed through the open door – or for an almost overpowering effect bring the pots indoors in the evening.

Oenothera The evening primroses need a light well-drained soil and revel in full sunshine, but are equally satisfied with light shade. As the name suggests, most open their flowers only in the evening, when the rich fragrance is given off, and this is true of the biennials which tend to produce flowers so fleeting that they are replaced almost daily. But the perennial kinds retain their flowers longer, hold them open all day and in return forfeit fragrance.

Oenothera biennis, a naturalised plant in many areas, opens its sweetly fragrant flowers between six and seven o'clock in the evening to announce its presence to evening flying moths, and blooms over several weeks in late summer. During the day the petals cleave to one another and withhold scent. Put it in a sunny corner near the house windows to benefit fully from its late show, or scatter the seeds where the flowers can be shown off against a dark background in the fading evening light. It is a true biennial.

Oenothera caespitosa is a scented perennial known as tufted evening primrose, whose white flowers bloom over a very long period from May to August with a sharp magnolia-like fragrance in the evening. This is a plant for the front of the border or a raised bed where its rather straggly habit is best accommodated. The individual flowers are exquisite, with pleated white petals deepening to pale rose pink with age, almost without stems and lying close to the plant. Propagate by division in spring.

Phlox paniculata is the scented border phlox so frequently grown in both town and country gardens. It needs a fertile, moisture-retentive soil in dappled shade for real success. Totally intolerant of drought, the leaves of the border phlox wilt at the thought of a hot dry week. Strongly perfumed, pervading the air around, the scent varies from day to day. This is because the freshly opened flowers are far sweeter in fragrance than the mature and fading ones. Their true value as garden plants rests in their flowering period, July to

The border phlox flowers from July to September. This is *Phlox paniculata* 'Leo Schlageter'

September, when so many other summer-flowering plants are beginning to go over. In carnival colours from white to purple to geranium red, the flowers are held in domed heads that add strong colour emphasis in the flower border.

Primula This vast genus offers some superbly scented plants for a variety of cultural situations. Velvety flowers painted in the richest of jewel colours and sometimes a combination of colours, provide good garden effect as well as demanding individual admiration. Some that flower early are invaluable with the spring-flowering bulbs and for bedding schemes, and the polyanthus in particular, where the paler-coloured flowers usually carry the best perfume. For waterside and woodland planting, several scented species are ideal. All form basal rosettes of leaves and can be raised from seed and often divided successfully. Most are completely hardy, and a few, notably the scented *Primula malacoides*, require greenhouse cultivation. *Primula viscosa*, a little rock garden plant, bears sweet-scented flowers but, unfortunately, evil-smelling sticky leaves.

Primula auricula has passed on its sweet honey-like perfume to all its derivatives over the centuries and the range of cultivated auriculas is now wide. Alpine auriculas, not seen as much as the border auriculas, are free from farina – the white meal that characteristically powders stem and calyces in the other sorts. Show auriculas are deliciously scented and are usually cultivated in pots and flowered under glass. Alpine auriculas may be used in the rock garden and flourish best tucked in behind a stone and facing north away from the direct sun. Give them some moisture-retentive material round their roots. Try a few plants at the front of a really shaded border among stones or in a made-up pocket of humus-rich soil or in a trough in the shade where the strong honeysuckle-like scent can be enjoyed.

Border auriculas bear the same rich scent too, but only share it when the atmosphere is really warm. Hardy and quite vigorous, they need a sunny spot in a soil that does not dry out in summer.

Primula florindae bears heavy bells of sulphur yellow (see p. 148)

Grey-green leaves with serrated edges are tempting to touch for their smoothness, and the flowers are richly coloured. Many of the cultivars have been grown for many years – one of the fancier's flowers, and deservedly so.

***Primula florindae*, the giant or Himalayan cowslip,** (see p. 147), is one of the tallest-growing species and loves to be near water. It will grow, but not as luxuriantly, in drier situations. Heavy yellow bells of sulphur yellow powdered with meal, flower in June and July with a rich cowslip scent.

Primula helodoxa is sometimes called 'glory of the marsh', which offers a clue to its cultural requirements. Lovely rich butter yellow flowers in June and July are sweetly fragrant and borne in tiers up the stem. It makes a very handsome plant dusted in creamy farina. Give it a place where it gets sunshine for part of the day.

Primula sikkimensis has large wrinkled leaves and stout stems that carry a cluster of pendent funnel-shaped flowers in June. Sweetly scented like cowslips, they are a strong pale yellow, frosted with meal within, and really one of the most distinctive of the primulas. Choose the damper parts of the garden for best results and treat it as a biennial, ensuring shelter from both cold winds and prolonged sunshine.

***Primula veris*, native cowslip,** bears a distinctive sweet scent which, unlike many other flowers, disappears once the flower has been pollinated. Rich yellow flowers with a flared mouth and rounded petals are distinguished, upon examination, by a tiny red spot at the base of each petal. Creamy green, dry-looking calyces behind them seem somewhat inflated. Propagate from seed and grow it in grass, particularly on neutral or slightly chalky soils, in the way it used to be found in English meadows.

Primula vialii looks more like a polygonum than a primula; the small violet-blue bells are tightly packed among scarlet calyces in a poker-like head and strongly fragrant. The bright green leaves in a rosette are upstanding, lending a slightly military air to the plant. It may be rather short-lived but can be raised from seed.

Viola A genus which is at its best in cool moist conditions where the creeping tufted growth will flourish in moisture-retentive leaf-mould. Some violets have been grown for hundreds of years, and have been known equally long for their ravishing scent. They are good plants for really shaded areas or to grow in troughs or containers where the scent can often be appreciated. Many people say that violets are not always scented, because the perfume quickly anaesthetises the nasal nerves, rendering them inactive. So the first sniff is delicious and then the fragrance appears to fade.

***Viola cornuta*, the alpine or horned violet,** has a tufted habit and blooms among its heart-shaped leaves from May to August. The flowers are a pale lavender blue (there is also a white form) and especially scented at dusk. It is the parent of several cultivars such as 'Arkwright's Ruby', bright crimson with a dark blotch. Use this viola and its forms at the front of the border in dappled shade.

***Viola odorata*, the sweet violet,** whose flowers cooked or crystallised were used to provide a sweetening alternative to honey in days gone by. Their prim little faces appear from January to May depending upon the season and locality (sometimes even starting to flower as early as November). Propagate by dividing the stolons in April, or from seed, which germinates best in cool conditions. Some scented cultivars are more free-flowering than the type, for instance 'Nellie Britton' (sometimes listed as 'Haslemere'), rosy mauve, 'Baroness de Rothschild', lavender blue and 'Czar', deep violet.

Viola odorata, the sweet violet

Trees and Shrubs

More than any other feature in the garden, trees and shrubs need to be assessed carefully before planting, for they are the principal long-lived forms that will establish the garden pattern. Ultimate space required, season of interest, and suitability to the site are all factors to be taken into account; the type-casting has to be accurate. But when planning the scented garden there is the added consideration of fragrance – some scents are dominant, some short-lived, some strongest in the evening, others overpowering with fishy overtones – so select with care.

Small trees from which to choose, all with white flowers, might include the eucryphias, good for sheltered sites, *Halesia carolina*, the snowdrop tree, delicately perfumed, and the more robust *H. monticola* with a slightly stronger scent. Also good is the lovely rounded head of *Ligustrum lucidum*, the wax-leaf privet which flowers in October with strongly scented cream flowers. More white flowers are produced by *Stewartia serrata*, richly fragrant at midsummer and then putting on a foliage carnival show in autumn. Some would include the sorbuses, too fishy for many noses, but all with creamy white flowers, or the elders, hawthorns and, where wall space allows, *Drimys winteri* for its rich white waxy flowers in June and fragrant bark for the remainder of the year. Even more white flowers come with the magnolias – *M. × soulangiana* and its cultivars, all happy suburban dwellers flowering in March and April, and the lovely lantern flowered *M. wilsonii* with its never-to-be-forgotten lemon fragrance.

The laburnum (best as *L. × watereri* 'Vossii' which does not produce poisonous seeds) bears golden yellow flowers in long tassels in June and is justifiably called golden rain. For red flowers, the hawthorn might perhaps be chosen, whilst *Malus hupehensis* and *M. coronaria* have pink flowers in spring and leaves turning richly flamboyant in autumn.

Among the shrubs possibilities include olearia, osmanthus, rhododendrons, the latter requiring plenty of space and acid soil conditions, otherwise they seem so out of place, and sarcoccoca for

Magnolia × soulangeana, white with a faint flush of pink

first-class ground cover and *Hamamelis* or *Stachyurus* for winter charm. Consider stephanotis for the greenhouse or conservatory, with plumbago, the hoyas and *Mandevilla laxa* (*suaveolens*). Climbers are invaluable in the scented garden: roses, jasmine, lonicera, some clematis, trachelospermum, climbing clerodendrons and wisteria, especially *W. sinensis*, the best fragrance of all in the long mauve tassels (see p. 165).

***Acacia dealbata*, wattle or the mimosa of florists,** is usually cultivated as a greenhouse or frost-free conservatory plant for very early spring flowering. In sheltered mild localities, such as those in the extreme south west of England, it is a tall shrub which may be grown outdoors against a sunny wall for protection. It loves the drought-like conditions at the base of a wall in a neutral to acid fertile soil. The buttercup yellow flowers are intoxicatingly fragrant of almond/violet and are carried in plumes of small fluffy balls. The foliage is feather-like, evergreen, and the growth somewhat lax. Propagate by seed, or from cuttings taken with a heel in summer.

Buddleja Buddlejas have a remarkable ability to attract butterflies, which, having once alighted, stay drunk with nectar. A lovely rich almond fragrance surrounds the flowers and drifts on the air also. Quick-growing, unfussy as to soil type, though perhaps happiest on the slightly more fertile soils, they flower when young; for quick results in the newly planted scented garden, plant one or two buddlejas. Propagate the kinds listed here by cuttings taken with a heel in late summer; *B. davidii* will also be successful from hardwood cuttings in autumn.

Buddleja alternifolia forms a large shrub eventually of weeping or arching habit, bedecked with mauve flowers in July and August, richly fragrant of heliotrope. Use it as a lawn specimen or high point in a small mixed border and watch the moths flutter about it in the evening.

***Buddleja davidii*, butterfly bush,** is probably – together with the richly scented elderberry – the most maltreated shrub of all, possibly because it is coarse-growing and quick to regenerate. Allow it plenty of room – its cane-like growth will peer over every fence – and choose a rubbly lime soil for best results. The buddleja will never fail, whatever the locality, to produce great arches of densely packed flowers in July and August which give off a rich musky honey-like fragrance. It is available in a range of flower colours through lavender and purple to rich burgundy, all of which are more fragrant than the white-flowered cultivars.

Buddleja fallowiana is a smaller and far more elegant shrub than *B. davidii* with similar flower and leaf form and a delicate fragrance. The stems and leaves are white and woolly, lending a frosted appearance and demanding some slight protection from winter dampness. Grow it in a sheltered position protected by a building or hedge where it can be seen against a darker background when in flower in July and early August.

Chimonanthus praecox, wintersweet, has sulphur yellow flowers strung along rather whippy branches in February and March. They blow a very sweet fragrance on to cold, dry air. A shrub to delight the nose just as the days lengthen; later, when the leaves appear, they are impregnated with a restrained version of the sweet fragrance. It is a medium-sized shrub to plant where it will get plenty of summer sunshine to ripen the wood. Propagate from cuttings taken in summer and then wait, because it is reluctant to flower when young. Choose a sheltered spot in a well-drained friable soil, chalky if possible.

Choisya ternata, Mexican orange blossom, so called because its lustrous evergreen leaves contain a rich spicy pungent orange scent released on crushing. The white flowers with a darker eye are gathered into clusters and have a far sweeter deep perfume like that of orange blossom. Summer is the main flowering time, but when it is happy, flowers will appear intermittently in flushes all year round. It is a medium to large shrub and a good hedge plant in the south of England, where it can be protected from wind chill, on a well-drained soil. Propagate in late summer by cuttings with a heel.

Cytisus The brooms have a reputation for being short-lived, but nevertheless their adaptability renders them immensely useful for the fragrant garden. They are sun worshippers, best on neutral fertile soil with good drainage, and flower when quite young with a wonderful outburst scenting the air around. Some smaller ones such as *C. purgans* with its upright habit are very sweetly scented and useful in tiny gardens or for cultivation in raised beds. In more extensive areas the arching branches of *C. × praecox*, the Warminster broom, will make fountains of sprays of sulphur yellow flowers early in summer – especially wonderful where several can

Cytisus battandieri flowers in July

be planted together as on a bank. Propagation is from cuttings (with a heel) after flowering, or from seed sown in spring.

Cytisus battandieri is one of the most handsome members of the broom family and clusters its flowers together into a long pineapple-shaped head, which is also strongly scented of pineapple. Set it in a corner or where it can gain shelter and encouragement from a house wall for its semi-evergreen foliage and soft woolly branches. It will soon reach to the top of a high wall. The flowers are bright yellow in erect heads in July and the silver branches are graceful and decorative for the remainder of the year.

Cytisus × spachianus is called the fragrant broom in spite of all its scented relatives. When allowed to grow naturally it is a tall spreading shrub, but often it is cultivated as a pot plant and marketed as 'Genista fragrans'. Grown this way it can be relied upon to give a first-class performance in late winter and early spring. The scent trapped in a conservatory or warm room is ravishing. Keep the growth cut back constantly to retain the bright jade green foliage.

Daphne The veriest amateur gardener knows of the thrill of the rich spicy scent of *Daphne odora* during bitterly cold February and March days, and this is only one of the family that can provide fragrance some time from November to June. Some are difficult, reluctant to stay, others are like spoiled children – choosing to behave only when it suits them. But they are tolerant of most soils, provided drainage is good and there is an all-the-year-round supply of humus enrichment. Buy in pots or transplant rooted cuttings direct to the flowering site because most daphnes transplant badly. Propagation is from heel cuttings taken in summer. Try the tiny *D. alpina* in the rock garden or in troughs for its sweet-scented white flowers in May, or *D. retusa*, a miniature with evergreen leaves, for a pan in the greenhouse, or a trough on the patio. It has waxy rose-purple flowers in May and June.

Daphne blagayana bears a rather elusive scent, but its rich creamy flowers in March and April are a delight. It is rather temperamental but a challenging plant for a good leafmould-rich soil in very light shade. When the straggling branches are buried, branch tips emerge to form a circle of dancing flowers around the bush. A treasure where it is happy.

Daphne × burkwoodii, (see p.165), is a fairly quick-growing shrub of medium height smothered in pale pink deliciously scented flowers in May. 'Somerset' is a selected and perhaps better form to grow.

Daphne cneorum, garland daphne or garland flower, (see p.165), is a delightful little shrubby plant for the rock garden, where it loves to have its feet in the shade and its head in the sun. Tight clusters of red buds open to starry-mouthed pink flowers in May and June. Slightly waxy in texture, their scent is ravishing. Often it repeats the flowering performance in very late summer and, as the polished foliage is evergreen, the plant is an asset all year round.

Daphne mezereum, best known for its highly polished red berries in summer, produces winter flowers in shades of mauvish pink to deep plum purple. In some areas they appear before Christmas, but generally the scent is associated with January and February, defying wind and rain with annual regularity. Select a wooded area for this winter treasure to trap the scent in the cold air.

Jasminum The jasmines are a versatile tribe of lax and climbing shrubs, all of which need constant tying in and frequent light pruning. The hardier ones tolerate town conditions and are not fussy as to soil provided that the drainage is good. Some, such as *J. polyanthum*, are best grown in a conservatory or porch where the scent can be retained and support provided for the pliant stems. Its long deep pink buds open to ravishingly scented blush white flowers which are produced very freely in early spring under glass, or a little later in really sheltered corners out of doors. For troughs or the rock garden try the miniature cushion forming *J. parkeri* with yellow richly sweet fragrant flowers in midsummer. Jasmines are propagated from stem cuttings taken with a heel after flowering.

Jasminum officinale, common jasmine, is a vigorous scrambler that loves to entwine with some other plant. Plant it in a mixed border where it has some shelter and part of the day in the shade, and give it a 'wigwam' of supports and encourage it to cover that. Although it will look pretty bleak in the winter the white summer flowers will compensate. A rich fragrance will drift over the border and the plant flowers continuously from midsummer to early autumn. It will also scramble over an arch at a doorway, where its scent can be enjoyed in passing.

Jasminum revolutum, a semi-evergreen for milder districts and town gardens, produces small, deep bright yellow flowers with rolled back petals from mid- to late summer. The gentle scent is one of the joys of the summer garden, and the plant does best on trellis or some support, or when it is allowed to grow through another plant. It does not object to being constantly restrained.

Ligustrum ovalifolium, common privet, is in fact so common as a hedge plant in older suburban gardens that its value in the decorative garden tends to be overlooked. Its golden-leaved form, 'Aureum', when allowed to grow naturally, is a handsome upright large shrub. Buttercup yellow leaves with bright green suffused along the central vein look good all summer, and are evergreen or semi-evergreen in all but the coldest areas. Creamy white small terminal flower panicles waft a heavy, almost sickly, rich scent across the garden in July. Privet is totally undemanding of soil provided it is not waterlogged; it accepts sun or shade, town and country, and can be relied upon to give of its best. Propagate from summer cuttings with a heel, or from hardwood cuttings, taken in autumn.

Lonicera, honeysuckles, are among the most rewarding of

Jasminum polyanthum on a conservatory porch

scrambling scented plants. They are highly decorative and the climbing sorts always twine from east to west. Choose dappled shade or a place that has shade for part of the day on well-drained soil in which some moisture retentive material has been incorporated. Encourage them to enfold the pillars of a pergola or unfurl over an arch or tripod of supports. They are invaluable for disguising posts or old tree stumps. When cut back and allowed to flop about, the common *L. periclymenum* will form a large dense scented mound, rather difficult to disentangle for pruning, but nevertheless providing good scented ground cover. The perfume is richest and strongest in the twilight when the long-tongued moths that fertilise the flowers are on the wing. Berries follow most flowers and seed forms in good summers, so propagation can be from seed when ripe but more commonly from late summer or autumn cuttings.

Lonicera fragrantissima, a medium-sized shrub, not a climber, comes into flower for the new year and continues until spring in all

Above: Honeysuckle, *Lonicera periclymenum* 'Belgica'
Below: *Mahonia* × *media* 'Charity' flowers in winter

but the vilest of winters. The foliage is leathery, semi-evergreen and decorated with creamy flowers in pairs, held back to back. As with many winter-flowering plants, a site that catches the early morning sunshine should be avoided.

Lonicera periclymenum, **common honeysuckle** of the hedgerows along with cultivated forms are winners in the garden and easy to manage. Long creamy white flowers in clusters are often flushed with purple-red on the outside, opening paler from June to September and even October in warm autumns. 'Belgica' with plum red flowers, and 'Serotina' with deep red in the flowers, are forms of *L. periclymenum* and are just as versatile and useful for their colour variation, retaining the powerful sweet fragrance.

Mahonia × media is the group name for hardy hybrids with stout stems from which a terminal cluster of flower stems radiate like spokes from an umbrella. They justly deserve a place near the house where the evergreen foliage and pale yellow flowers smelling of lily-of-the-valley can be enjoyed in winter. Good fragrant cultivars include 'Charity' and 'Winter Sun'. The mahonias like semi-shade and most good friable soil types, and are particularly useful for covering banks and as informal hedges. Propagation is from seed when ripe, layers in spring, or summer cuttings of stem tips.

Myrtus communis, **common myrtle,** when grown out of doors in a sheltered locality produces an abundance of white starry flowers with fluffy centres in May and June (see p. 130). The whole plant is richly and delicately scented, and the foliage aromatic, but liable to damage from cold winds and frost. It is particularly good in seaside gardens, and a lovely scented plant for the conservatory or garden room when grown in a tub in potting compost. It is a plant that will thrive in town gardens too, and adapts to most soils including chalk. Propagate from cuttings taken with a heel in summer and give some heat to encourage rooting.

Philadelphus, **mock oranges,** are a floriferous tribe of medium to large shrubs with a tendency to lax growth. The foliage is pale green and there is a general air of gentleness about them. The white flowers, abundantly borne, are powerfully scented of orange blossom and are so generous with it that the whole garden can be dominated by it being carried on the breeze. A place in full sunshine on dry soils suits them best and by careful selection of species and hybrids the period of flower can be extended considerably from May until July. Try the cultivars of *P. × lemoinei* like 'Avalanche' for their decorative flowers which literally weigh down the arching branches. Propagation is from hardwood cuttings of ripened wood in autumn or summer cuttings with a heel. Seed is produced, but does not breed true.

Philadelphus coronarius is the most fragrant-flowered species, and one of the most popularly grown, especially in its golden leaved form 'Aureus'. It is a good plant with which to lighten up a border, even a shaded one, and the leaves quieten down to a pale green-gold as summer progresses. The flowers are creamy white, weighing down the whole branch in June.

Rosa Fragrance is the universal appeal of roses. As climbers or shrubs there are numerous ways in which they can be incorporated into the decorative garden scheme. In general the climbers will enjoy more shade than the bush types and they all love a moisture-retaining soil containing a good supply of humus. More than any other plant roses display an enormous range of scent within the 'rose' spectrum – from fruity to tarry, to tea, to lemon, to spicy, while many more nuances are detectable. The species are the oldest roses in cultivation and are among the richest in scent. *Rosa centifolia*, the cabbage rose, with its full rounded flowers, is deeply rose-scented and its forms such as 'Fantin Latour', a lovely pale pink, and 'Tour de Malakoff', magenta-mauve, retain the sweet full-bodied perfume. The damask rose, *R. damascena*, provides a gentle true rose perfume; try it in its forms 'Comte de Chambord', 'Marie Louise' and 'Celsiana', all pink. Some roses have not only fragrant flowers but also deliciously scented foliage. This is so in *R. rubiginosa*, the eglantine or sweet briar, a rose to plant so that the prevailing breeze will carry the aroma towards the house on a warm evening after rain – nothing could be more perfect. The arching branches are very prickly and bedecked with red hips in autumn. 'Lord Penzance', pollen yellow; 'Lady Penzance', copper gold; 'Amy Robsart', strong pink; and 'Meg Merrilees', crimson, are all favourite *rubiginosa* forms with delicately fragrant flowers.

Bourbon roses are free-flowering and some are fragrant over a long period from June to September. Some suggestions of varieties to plant are: 'La Reine Victoria', rose pink and true rose-scented; and 'Mme Isaac Periere', deep rose red and scented of raspberries.

Above: *Rosa filipes* 'Kiftsgate', a vigorous climber
Below: *Rosa centifolia* 'Fantin Latour'

Cluster-flowered roses (floribundas) are sometimes devoid of scent but one or two may be included in the fragrant garden – 'Ma Perkins' for example, pink with a true rose perfume; 'Victoriana', tangerine/silver; and 'Golden Fleece', yellow and also smelling of raspberries.

The musk roses are vigorous shrubs which carry dense trusses of flower followed by innumerable glossy hips and are therefore good for autumn effect with the remarkably attractive foliage. Select 'Buff Beauty', apricot with an intense rose scent; 'Penelope', cream with a musky rose scent; and 'Felicia', pale silvery pink and spiced with an aromatic tang.

The large-flowered roses (hybrid teas) are legion, thoroughly deserving their popularity, but for fragrance try such as 'Doris Tysterman', tangerine; 'Fragrant Cloud', coral-scarlet; 'Papa Meilland', crimson; 'Super Star', vermilion; 'Troika', amber; 'Whisky Mac', golden orange; and 'Blue Moon', lavender (not to everyone's taste for colour, but lemon-scented). A few miniature roses have fragrant flowers and are useful for the rock garden edge, troughs, walls or in pots; 'Sweet Fairy', pale mauve; 'Yellow Doll', pale yellow, and the white 'Twinkles' are all scented.

Of sterling value in the scented garden are the climbing and rambler roses, for they lift the scent up to the air and they combine well with all kinds of other garden plants, which bush roses do not do as happily. Many are especially useful when grown on walls, where the scent is enormously enhanced in the evening by the reflected heat from the wall which keeps the temperatures up to coax even more perfume out of them. Fragrance rather than the classification of type is the concern here for there are numerous hybrids and cultivars, sports and species of climbing habit. Some are good in one situation, others in another and they are used to clothe fences, walls, arches, pergolas and posts or to fling up into an old tree, to festoon an arbour, camouflage a shed or decorate a balustrade. One or two to look out for are *Rosa filipes* 'Kiftsgate', vigorous, white-flowered and smelling of incense; *R. laevigata*, the Cherokee rose, deep cream and spicy; 'New Dawn', shell pink and enticingly fruity; 'Paul Lédé', apricot-buff and smelling like tea; 'Zéphirine Drouhin', soft rose pink and sweetly scented; 'Goldfinch', yellow fading to cream and strongly scented; and 'Veilchenblau', lavender-blue-grey-mauve and scented of oranges (plant it where it can be shown off against a light background).

It is nearly impossible to select 'the best' for the fragrant garden but for special interest the following are recommended (see also the Wisley Handbook, *Roses*).

Rosa centifolia 'Muscosa', the moss rose, is a small shrub in which the scent glands can be seen on the backs of the petals and as a soft bristly green growth on stems and calyces. Even when the flowers are in bud the moss-like growth releases a resinous scent which is retained on the skin. There is a slightly oily feel to the flower head and the fragrance is full and richly rose-scented. A good plant for the small garden, and nice in the forms 'Mousseline', for its intense scent, or 'William Lobb', with a truly captivating rose perfume.

Rosa banksiae 'Lutea', yellow Banksian rose, outstrips many others in its race up the house wall, and produces a myriad of tiny yellow double flowers quite early in the summer. Grow it where space allows, for its delightful violet scent.

Rosa gallica var. *officinalis*, the rose of Provins or apothecaries' rose, although prone to suckering, is one to introduce for fragrance, especially where space allows this small spreading bush to be planted *en masse* – or to make an informal hedge. It is best of all for drying the petals to incorporate into *pot pourri* for they retain all the fullness of their scent. Deep red semi-double flowers appear in June, on low bushes that can be regularly pruned hard and will regenerate with vigour. For a true rose perfume with all its depth and enchantment, 'Belle de Crécy' is the form to grow, with its magenta pink flowers fading to crimson and parma violet.

Syringa The common lilac has been grown in our gardens since the sixteenth century and forms a tall upright deciduous shrub well known for its strong scent. It was introduced from the mountainous regions of eastern Europe and the Middle East, along with the highly scented *Philadelphus* (see p. 159). In common parlance the two have been confused ever since; the one, *Philadelphus*, being known by the name *Syringa* of the other. The lilacs are unselective of soil, but show perhaps a little preference for chalk, and grow equally well in both town and country. Some of the species are highly fragrant and the rose-pink flowered hybrid *S. × josiflexa* (*S. josikaea × S. reflexa*), raised in Canada, particularly so. The Rouen lilac, *S. × chinensis*, with drooping flower panicles of soft lavender is heavily fragrant and has been known in cultivation for about two hundred years. Propagation is from summer cuttings taken with a heel, or hardwood cuttings in autumn.

Syringa × persica, **Persian lilac or blue Persian jasmine,** claims attention for the smaller garden, as it forms a small rounded

Rosa gallica var. *officinalis*, the apothecaries' rose

graceful shrub decked with typical lilac-shade fragrant flowers in dainty panicles in May. Best protected from cold winds, it is otherwise a gem. The scent is light and distinctly spicy.

Syringa vulgaris, common lilac, provides a host of cultivars with heavy panicles of flowers in May varying in colour from white through mauve to deep plum red. They are richly but variously scented, wonderful after rain, and good summer screening shrubs especially useful in town and suburban gardens. Old flower heads ought to be removed but rarely are, and pruning is neglected also, but still the shrubs flower with unfailing regularity. Good heart-shaped clean green leaves make a dense foil for the flowers. Cultivars are numerous, but some well-tried ones are: 'Congo', deep velvety purple flowers in rather dumpy heads; 'Mme Lemoine', top-of-the-milk cream in bud and pure white double flowers; 'Charles Joly', another with double flowers in plum red and flowering rather late; and 'Ambassadeur', blue-mauve flowers with a white eye.

Above: *Wisteria sinensis* flowers in May (see p. 152)
Below left: *Daphne cneorum* flowers in late spring (see p. 155)
Below right: *Daphne × burkwoodii* 'Somerset' (see p. 155)

165

Viburnum Many viburnums bear flowers strongly scented of honey and the deciduous ones follow with a good autumn display of shining berries and startling foliage. Viburnums dislike a peaty soil, but are happy in most situations and tolerate seaside gardens and town gardens alike; *V.* × *burkwoodii*, especially, seems to thrive among town buildings. Propagation is from cuttings with a heel, taken after flowering for the deciduous ones, and in early summer for the evergreen ones.

Viburnum × **burkwoodii,** an evergreen, is one of the most useful medium-sized shrubs for winter flowers. Encrusted flower heads of deep pink buds appear about the new year, open to white with a really sweet scent, and go on into April and May.

Viburnum *carlesii* forms a small rounded deciduous bush with often particularly good autumn colour. It is deservedly popular for its ease of cultivation. The flowers are sweetly daphne-like or spicy in scent, and bloom in April and May. Buds are rosy pink, and open slowly to give pure white flower heads.

Viburnum *farreri* **(V. *fragrans*),** which Reginald Farrer called 'the most glorious of shrubs', is another winter-flowering plant. The foliage is attractively bronzed when young and the pink bud clusters turn to white on opening. They often manage to do this before Christmas and go on for some time during the darkest days of the winter. They are richly scented with a spicy overtone.

Wisteria sinensis forms a rather gawky shrub, seen at its best when supported by a wall or pergola or allowed to grow over a shed or summerhouse. Then the long tassel-like mauve flowers can hang down among the filmy decorative foliage. Plant it somewhere where its nakedness is masked in winter to spare its awkwardness, and provided there is some moisture-retentive material deep round the roots it will outlive two or three generations. The flowers in May are fragrant of vanilla when the entire plant assumes a likeness to a Chinese painting on silk. Propagation is from summer cuttings with a heel and some heat.

Bulbs and Corms

One of the very best investments for the garden is bulbous plants, provided that good-quality material is selected. Once planted in a suitable position, most of them look after themselves, giving pleasure for years, and even increasing in number. The most widely cultivated are those suitable for mass planting. Early spring holds much of the garden excitement for scent when bulbs have been planted of narcissus, crocus, muscari, snowdrops and iris. However, beginners often fail to realise that autumn-flowering species of snowdrops, crocus and cyclamen are also available. Careful perusal of catalogues, or advice from specialist firms will suggest further ideas. (See the Wisley Handbook, *Growing Dwarf Bulbs*.)

Out of doors the scent of plants that bloom in the cold dim days of winter is often lost on the wind, or can really only be enjoyed by close inspection. So plant *Crocus chrysanthus* 'Snow Bunting' and miniature narcissus, such as *Narcissus* 'Silver Chimes', and the honey-scented snowdrops like *Galanthus* 'Magnet' or 'Straffan' in troughs near an entrance to the house or garage where they may be enjoyed.

Often the mad March winds coincide with the flowering of some of the scented plants such a narcissus, muscari, *Iris reticulata* and *I. histrioides*, but where space allows, if these are planted in drifts, the somewhat elusive scent will be sensed occasionally. All can be cultivated in pots, troughs, or window boxes to give their special delights.

As for summer-flowering bulbs, lilies probably claim the accolade for scent, but galtonia, summer irises such as *Iris florentina* and *I. pallida* and pancratium are all worth a place in even the smallest garden.

One great joy of bulbs is that they can be grown in pots. The right growing conditions can be given, and they will reward with unblemished highly fragrant flowers in the conservatory, porch, living room or on a loggia or patio in summer. They can be transported from place to place to give the right colour emphasis in a summer flower border – lilies can be used in this way – and they can even be given or lent to friends, hospital patients or used for church decoration.

Galtonia candicans flowers in July and August

Crocus Crocuses are undoubtedly at their best when naturalised beneath trees or among shrubs, but a few at the edge of the lawn where they can be enjoyed during the short winter days, when the sun coaxes them to open, are a delight. Unselective of soil, they are so defenceless against mice and birds!

Crocus ancyrensis is one of the first scented crocuses to flower, probably in time for the new year, and it will startle with its yellow spears that burst into glowing tangerine in the slightest ray of warmth from the sun. Put it in a spot that catches the early afternoon sun, for this one reason.

Crocus chrysanthus usually flowers by mid-February except in particularly harsh winters, and is the parent of a wide range of seedlings such as 'Blue Giant' and the purple and white 'Ladykiller'. But the best for scent is the pure white 'Snow Bunting', feathered and streaked with purple.

Galanthus Numerous garden forms, quite indistinguishable to all but the practised eye, have a refreshing spring-like scent reminiscent of primroses. Although by selecting the forms and species, snowdrops can be in flower from October to April or even May, they are beloved for their toughness and purity during the worst of the wintry weather.

They cannot be described as richly scented, but that spring freshness is a mossy scent on the cold air, and one or two are slightly violet-scented. They are harbingers of spring that hate the soil to be fed; if you wish to move them, they are best divided just as the flowers are fading.

Galanthus nivalis is probably a native British plant, with narrow strap-shaped leaves and globular white flowers that dangle by the merest thread from the top of their individual stem. Varieties such as 'Magnet' and 'Straffan' are distinctly honey-scented.

Galtonia candicans produces white trumpet-like bells tinged with green all around a $2\frac{1}{2}$ ft (75 cm) stem in July and August. It is perhaps seen at its best in a sunny sheltered site in humus-rich well-drained soil where it is allowed to develop good clumps. These may need covering in the winter, as it is a South African plant. Its real value as a scented plant is after the stems have been cut and arranged in water, for then the fragrance strengthens. A lovely plant for church flowers for an August wedding.

Hyacinthus orientalis forms are nowadays limited to the bold compact clusters of flowers held on fat straight stems, and displaying no resemblance to the species. The common hyacinth is seen at its best when forced in pots or bowls. Because the double-flowered forms do not force as well, they are not offered for sale as readily. When grown in bowls a good fibrous bulb compost should be used and the bulbs close planted in September or October. A deep rich fertile soil and a position sheltered from the wind are needed for success out of doors, when bulbs should be planted almost 5 in. (12.5 cm) deep in September or October. They need to be lifted each year after flowering, unlike most bulbs. The scent is penetrating, heavy and sweet. Some popular varieties from which to choose are 'L'Innocence', white; 'Myosotis', blue and particularly richly scented; 'Lady Derby', pink; 'Yellow Hammer', yellow; and 'Cherry Blossom', red.

Iris Most irises appreciate open sunny positions, where the drainage is good and there is at least a smattering of lime in the soil. Some are rather reluctant to flower, but those listed here should not present difficulties for the average gardener, especially when one's efforts are reinforced by good summers to 'bake' the iris clumps after flowering. The great rainbow range of cultivars of *Iris germanica*, or bearded iris, have a rich fruity scent which thickens and changes once the stems are cut and arranged indoors.

Iris histrioides defies the elements to bloom from mid-January onward, with gorgeous deep blue spiky flowers marked with gold that nestle close to the ground. For this reason alone, it is best to cultivate this iris in pots and bring them into the garden room or porch where the cool sweet perfume can develop and be enjoyed from time to time. The form 'Major' is usually grown, with ultramarine blue flowers and black and golden markings.

Iris florentina provides the scented orris root of commerce, and is a plant of ancient cultivation. The roots possess the fragrance of violets, which strengthens as they dry after lifting. The flowers in May and June are white tinged with lavender with a golden yellow beard on the falls, and sword-like leaves. A good mid-to-front of the border plant which will make a fine clump if left undisturbed.

Iris pallida is known for its sweetly scented flowers although, because it is frequently seen in cultivation in its variegated leaf form, it is probably considered first for its decorative foliage. The

Iris reticulata flowers in winter

two forms with coloured leaves are 'Aurea Variegata' and 'Argentea Variegata', both with pale blue flowers but with a strong vanilla scent.

Iris reticulata, a winter-flowering species, is totally reliable, producing its curiously upstanding blue-mauve flowers in the severest of winters. It is a good plant for the rock garden, trough or for bowls in the conservatory; grown in crocus bowls (with planting holes all round) and brought indoors, this iris makes a delightful violet-scented table decoration. Choose a really well-drained spot for outdoor cultivation and grow 'Cantab', with pale blue flowers, or 'J. S. Dijt', plum purple.

Iris unguicularis (see back cover) is a winter favourite which unfortunately hides its pale lavender-blue flowers among its papery leaves. If you gather the blooms and bring them into a warm room, they will give off their violet scent and bring spring freshness to a January day. Plant at the foot of a wall, especially where it can be

Lilium regale has very fragrant white flowers (see p. 175)

sun-baked during the summer, and forget it for years. That is the best encouragement to flowering.

Lily The amateur gardener often regards the cultivation of lilies as something of a challenge, but by careful selection, i.e. suitability to site, or cultivation in pots, good results can be assured. Not all lilies are scented, but those that are usually emit a strong rich scent, even too strong for some tastes. When grown in pots or tubs the bulbs need to be planted deeply if they are stem-rooting lilies like *Lilium auratum*, and just to nose depth otherwise. Good drainage is essential and any good proprietary compost will suit them. Leave enough space at the top of the container to allow for top dressing with additional compost later. Buy from reliable sources, preferably in October, and the fleshy-scaled bulbs ought to be plump and firm. The great advantage of growing lilies in pots is that they can be moved about the garden and patio when in flower to gain the best effect and full enjoyment of their luscious flowers.

Lilium auratum lives up to its popular name of golden-rayed lily by producing abundant very large white flowers broadly decorated with a band of waxy gold along each petal. It is normally late-flowering, so is best grown in a pot, to get an early start to growth. Several hybrids are available, all richly endowed with spicy scent, and they flower over a considerable period in the late summer. Good on acid soils where sharp drainage can be provided together with shelter from prevailing winds.

Lilium candidum, madonna lily, is best when grown in borders where it can be left undisturbed for a number of years. Find it a spot where it can stand in the shade and hold its head in the sun. The glistening pure white flowers, assembled in a cluster at the top of the stem, are decorated with bright golden anthers and an almost overpowering honey scent – too strong for some people. This is perpetuated in its descendants, the Cascade Hybrids. After flowering the bulbs are dormant for only a short period, and need to be planted or transplanted in August.

Lilium henryi is one of the easiest lilies to grow, especially on chalky soil. It gives a display of deep apricot orange flowers spotted prominently with brown. Sometimes there are as many as 40 or 50

Lilium auratum has a spicy scent

Lilium henryi is an easy lily to grow

flowers to a stem in July or August. The sweet scent is particularly lingering and has found its way into the range of Aurelian Hybrids which have *L.henryi* in their parentage.

Lilium longiflorum, the Easter lily of florists' shops, is a good cool greenhouse plant where it can be gently forced, and never fails to bloom in March and April. But out of doors, in sheltered areas the flowers come in high summer when the evenings are long and the jasmine scent can be enjoyed. A good 'special event plant' for a border near house or patio; but doubtfully hardy. Best in the variety *takesima* with somewhat grander pure white trumpets up to 6 in. (15 cm) long. A number of named varieties are available, the best perhaps 'Croft' and 'White Queen'.

Lilium parryi revels in dappled shade and is good for an open woodland planting. Its clear yellow funnel-shaped flowers stand up well against darker backgrounds. It is a lily of exceptional grace, flowering in May and June.

Lilium regale is one of the easiest of lilies to grow, and is justifiably popular. Lime-tolerant, it likes a sunny spot where its roots are protected by its neighbours from winter frosts, which suggests a shrub border as an ideal site. The white flowers are strongly fragrant, funnel-shaped and flushed brown and maroon pink on the outside and deep golden yellow at the throat within (see p. 172).

Muscari Leave muscari bulbs undisturbed for four or five years so that the colonies will build up, then divide them. They are most attractive when planted together with other bulbs and naturalised under deciduous trees or shrubs, for they love every ray of winter sunshine. These plants are tolerant of lime, but happy on any soil but the coldest of clay. Their grass-like leaves usually peep through in autumn.

Muscari armeniacum is a really easy plant, thriving equally well in town and country gardens. In April and early May the deep blue flowers edged with white are knotted about the head of the stem. The form 'Cantab' is popularly available, with slightly paler blue flowers and the same sweet fragrance. Planted in a pocket on the rock garden or as a ribbon edge to a border or path, it cannot fail to attract attention. It is not too demanding as to sunlight; semi-shade appears to satisfy its needs.

Muscari moschatum is the most sweetly perfumed of the muscaris, with a musk-like overtone, as its specific name implies. Perfectly hardy in a sunny position, it has rather dusky purple green flowers (that are not to everyone's liking!) which turn to a golden olive green lower down the stem on maturity. It blooms in April, with leaves rather broader than those described as grass-like.

Narcissus The name narcissus relates to *narc* – a dullness of sense – from whence is derived the word 'narcotic'. This is because in some forms the perfume of narcissus induces headaches and giddiness when deeply inhaled. Ordinary daffodils are undoubtedly the most popular bulbs for naturalising in grass, among shrubs or in woodland areas, and yet they are equally effective when cultivated in pots, tubs, window boxes or even old wheelbarrows! Symbolic of the English spring, some of the flowers are strongly scented, others not. Most seem to prefer the meadow/woodland type of soil and many of the small ones are happy where drainage is better, for example, in the rock garden or in troughs.

Garden cultivars of narcissus are divided into twelve divisions, dependent upon the type of flower. All have a fresh spring earthiness about them, but some have a deliciously rich scent, sometimes quite overpowering. Bulb catalogues are a good guide to the innumerable cultivars available and usually record the scent. All narcissus bulbs need to be planted early; August is not too soon, as the new roots start to grow again in the late summer. (See the Wisley Handbook, *Daffodils*.)

Jonquillas, suited to cultivation in sheltered areas out of doors, or in pots in the conservatory or indoors, are perhaps the strongest of all in their perfume. The fragrance is quite distinctive, rich and spicy, and the golden yellow flowers with short cups are carried in little clusters at the head of the stem.

Narcissus juncifolius in the same group is a delightful miniature species, with dark rush-like leaves and tiny yellow flowers in clusters in March and April. It is ideal for cultivating in pans in the cold greenhouse or in a trough by a sheltered patio or a scree bed or pocket in the rock garden.

N. poeticus are the latest flowering of all the spring-flowering narcissi and sometimes get overlooked for this reason, coming during the plenteousness of the fragrant plants of May. Plant the bulbs in groups and leave them undisturbed and their chalk-white petals and crushed flat cups of pure gold, tangerine or yellow will provide gorgeous cut flowers with good stems for many years.

Tazettas are sweet-scented, bunch-flowered 'narcissi' which in the very mildest areas can be persuaded into flower out of doors for the new year. The popular 'Paperwhite', known to florists for the Christmas market, can be cultivated in bowls, or even in clean water, indoors, in a bowl of pebbles to anchor the roots. The scent will fill the room. 'Geranium', 'Soleil d'Or', and 'Cragford', with frilly cups, can be grown out of doors in mild places, and are excellent for forcing.

Pancratium illyricum is an unusual summer-flowering bulb, and one for those amateur gardeners who wish to try something a little different and challenging – best perhaps in a cold frame, or in a made-up bed in a sheltered spot in towns and other mild areas. Star-like fragrant white flowers, with tufted stamens and resembling daffodils in shape, appear in May and June. In autumn plant the large pear-shaped bulbs deeply for winter protection.

Aromatic Plants

Aromatic plants are the custodians of the richest and probably the most complex of essential oils, locking them away within the plant itself. Leaves often need to be crushed or rubbed to persuade the plant to release them to the nose. For the most part aromatic fragrances are subtle, less flowery in quality than flower scents, and are usually only discernible during the summer months even in some evergreen plants.

Herbs fall into this category, cultivated for centuries for their essential oils as flavouring and perfume, and while they may not be among the stars of the garden, they provide a valuable back-up chorus line, rich in fragrance. Their close association with man is recorded in the general use of their common English names – their scientific names seem somewhat unfamiliar: *Balsamita*, costmary, alecost or camphor plant, with minty-camphor-like fragrance and smooth leaves; *Myrrhis*, sweet cicely; *Levisticum*, lovage, with its earthy celery-like flavour and smell; and *Ruta*, rue, a good border plant with blue-green foliage, bitter in the extreme, but bearing yellow flowers that try to compensate by pretending to be cowslip in their scent. Other aromatic plants like the *Cistus* or rock rose produce their scent from the oily glandular hairs of the leaves, and some of them are even called gum cistuses. Conifers also are resinous, displaying a range of scent and always enhanced by a warm moist day.

Some green aromatics only really assume their real fragrance upon drying; *Galium odoratum*, woodruff, is one of these. Their place in the scented garden is assured, however, because they are lovely garden plants in themselves. And what could be more rewarding to the gardener, during a summer evening stroll round the garden, than to find a plant which, when touched in recognition, gives its scent in return?

Aloysia triphylla (A. citriodora, Lippia citriodora), lemon verbena, is claimed to have the leaves with the strongest aroma. It survives out of doors tucked into a corner or sheltered border where there is a dry root run, in the milder localities, otherwise it is a good conservatory plant to grow in a container. Long narrow shining green leaves are highly fragrant of lemon, which they surrender when broken or rubbed. Propagate by cuttings in summer.

Artemisia Artemisias are perennials grown for their decorative aromatic foliage, and the scent is generally refreshing and sweet. Use them in the flower border to cool down the colour effects, or grow them beside a frequently used path where they can be handled often to release the fragrance. They all appreciate a friable soil and sunshine. Culinary French tarragon is a form of *A. dracunculus* which lacks the sweetness of most artemisias.

Artemisia abrotanum, southernwood or old man, is a shrubby cottage garden plant with silky thread-like foliage with a crisp sweet camphor-like aroma. It is horribly gnarled in winter, so tuck it among better looking companions and cut it back in the spring to encourage new growth.

Artemisia absinthium, wormwood, is a delightful plant forming a rounded medium-sized bush in a good moisture-retentive soil with its head in the sun. Silver green-grey leaves, with a tinge of apple green overall, shaped like little hands are sweetly fragrant with camphor overtones. Decked with dew or raindrops the whole plant is magic and the scent will linger about it. Cut it back judiciously to keep the fresh foliage going for the best scent. Add a few leaves to *pot pourri*.

Artemisia chamaemelifolia, lady's maid, is a gentle plant, with green finely cut foliage that holds a sharp sweet camphor-like aroma when it is bruised. A good edging plant, because it tolerates clipping, it is also effective when used in block planting.

Artemisia pontica, Roman wormwood, has a very clean camphor-mint aroma held in delicate foliage. The leaves are feathery and thread-like on twiggy upstanding stems. Good for ground cover in both sun and shade and particularly useful for awkward banks that can be given over to the one plant. Its rhizomes run about just below the surface so keep it well away from border favourites.

Artemisia tridentata has small three-pointed dull grey wedge-shaped leaves, which crowd together in clusters. It has a truly sweet aroma, outstanding even among the artemisias, and gives it up so easily on the surrounding air, but it is invasive.

Chamaemelum nobile, Roman chamomile, often catalogued as *Anthemis nobilis*, is a useful plant because its tough jointed stems grow prostrate and so the plants are mat-forming. A perennial of

Artemisia abrotanum, southernwood or old man

ancient cultivation, it is still popularly used for making chamomile tea from the aromatic flowers. The thread-like leaves are also rich in aromatic oils. Its somewhat ragged appearance is compensated by its delicious apple fragrance and it tolerates being walked on so is invaluable in making scented paths and lawns. Grow the non-flowering kind called 'Treneague' for these purposes, or to clothe a bank behind a seat. Rooted stems need to be planted in friable stone-free and well-drained soil in April about 4 to 6 in. (10–15 cm) apart to form a 'mat'.

***Foeniculum vulgare*, fennel,** is a superbly graceful plant with finely cut foliage in soft plumes. When bruised these leaves give off a strong anise-like smell. It is a tall plant with an unusual soft feathery shape and is especially decorative in the form entirely suffused with a rich black purple bronze. The flowers are yellow in dainty flat heads in June and July, but to keep the aroma sweet and also to avoid excessive self-seeding, cut away the flowering stems when the buds form. Sow seed in spring or divide established roots in September and give fennel a sunny spot in a well-drained soil. It is usually a kitchen or herb garden plant, but of considerable worth in the flower border for both its foliage colour and form.

Helichrysum serotinum is redolent of curry, hence its popular name of curry plant. It is a perennial with a woody base and likes a position in the front of the border or across a bank where it can enjoy full sunshine. In the decorative border its needle-like silver foliage has a role to play, especially after rain or dew when it sparkles like tinsel. Dingy yellow flowers on rather straggly stems in July and August do nothing to endear it. Its curry supper smell travels quite a distance when the atmosphere is warm.

***Hyssopus officinalis,* hyssop,** is an aromatic shrubby little perennial which is evergreen in the milder localities and in the south of the country. The leaves are tiny, dark green and lock away its spicy fragrance until the warmth of summer. The aroma is at its richest as the tiny flowers appear in June. It is useful as a front of the border plant in a sunny spot and tolerant of dry conditions, but invaluable as a container plant throughout the year. The tiny snapdragon-like flowers are fleeting and sparse, usually blue but there are pink- and white-flowered forms. It is a lovely old-world plant to enjoy for its fragrance.

Lavandula stoechas, French lavender, flowers in summer

Lavandula The lavenders are valuable garden plants cultivated since ancient times for their unique refreshing fragrance which permeates both leaves and flower bracts. They prefer good drainage and full sunshine away from frost pockets but even so are short-lived. Chalky soils seem to encourage a richness of perfume. Propagation is from cuttings taken in early summer and it is a good idea to maintain a supply of rooted cuttings to replace any losses in winter and to use in containers such as tubs and window boxes.

***Lavandula angustifolia (L. spica, L. officinalis),* old English lavender,** is instantly recognised for its mound of grey foliage pricked all over in July and August by mauve flower heads which resemble pins in the pincushion. A well grown established plant is richer in scent than a young one and, as with most other aromatic plants, the essential oils are richest just before the flowers mature. This is the time to gather flowers for *pot pourri* and other fragrant conceits. Various forms of lavender are a variation on a theme: 'Grappenhall', with large pale mauve flowers; 'London Pink', pale pink; 'Munstead' (sometimes marketed as 'Munstead Dwarf'), good purple flowers on a compact plant; 'Hidcote', dark purple; and 'Twickel Purple', purple and the leaves set at right angles to the stem, with perhaps the best of all lavender perfumes.

***Lavandula stoechas,* French lavender,** is a smaller less splendid plant with green-grey leaves and 'hat pin' flower heads with prominent persistent bracts. The scent is far more oily and herby than that of *L. angustifolia,* which reminds us that lavender is an ancient antiseptic. It demands a really sheltered spot and is a truly short-lived perennial. Grow it in a container, and give it some winter shelter to help it through the worst winter weather. Propagation is from summer cuttings.

***Melissa officinalis,* lemon balm,** (see p. 183), is a true English cottage garden plant, important for the bee keeper and sometimes known as bee balm. In Tudor times it was grown as a strewing herb. It is one of the aromatic plants that retains its rich lemony fragrance after cutting, and dries well. Good rounded bushes solid in appearance are formed, so that melissa looks well at either side of a gateway or as a 'corner stone' of flower borders. The leaves are tough, nettle-like in shape and at their most decorative in the variegated form, 'Variegata', when they are painted with a clear yellow. The form 'Aurea' has an even more golden leaf area. Both are excellent for shade as they do not lose their colouring, although they much prefer a sunny spot with a good moisture retentive soil. If they dry out on light soils or during particularly dry summers, the aroma will deteriorate and take on a distinctly musty and stale overtone. Try growing it in tubs where the soil condition can be controlled. Little white flowers, rather detracting from the plant, appear in June and July. Propagation is best from cuttings of new growth taken in May as seed is slow to germinate. Cut back growth at the end of the summer to encourage a fresh crisply aromatic renewal the following spring.

Mentha The range of aromas is wide in the various mint plants and is matched only by their numerous English names. Most are outrageously invasive and unselective of soil, although they do need to have some moisture-retentive element to produce a clean fresh aroma. Late in the season and in dry summers their scent becomes very musty. All parts of the plant are impregnated by the aroma throughout the year. Propagation is usually very easily effected by breaking away a shoot or two with the creeping stem and a few roots. All the mints have a slightly military air and despotic intentions, so confine the roots in some way – bricks or slates pushed into the ground palisade-fashion are effective. The most refreshing clean scent of all is in M. *spicata*, spearmint, of the kitchen garden and used for mint sauce. None have remarkable flowers; they all form spikes of mauve or pink blooms and it is advisable to remove flowering stems to preserve the aroma at its best.

Mentha × *gentilis* **'Variegata', ginger mint or Scotch mint,** marches about but it is useful for its lettuce-green leaves with golden yellow suffused about the veins. They are warmly pungent of ginger when rubbed. Put it at the front of the border, where it can be restrained in passing.

Mentha × *piperita*, **peppermint** and its forms, variously comprise eau de cologne mint, orange mint and bergamot mint, and herein lies the key to the fact that the composition of the essential oils varies imperceptibly, suggesting one scent today and another tomorrow. A plant grown in one situation may have a completely different scent to one grown elsewhere, but is always an interesting nuance of aroma. Often the leaves are rather heart-shaped and swirl around the square stem. M. × *piperita citrata* is highly fragrant and refreshing and has the reputation of enhancing the fragrance of its

Melissa officinalis 'Variegata', lemon balm (see p. 181), has lemon-scented leaves and is a vigorous herbaceous perennial

neighbours. The lovely jade green stems of *M. × officinalis*, white peppermint, add a decorative contrast to any collection of mints.

Mentha pulegium, pennyroyal, makes a tiny-leaved mat-forming plant, useful to put pools of growth into a scented path, or to make a patch of mint-scented lawn. Pungent and peppery in aroma, it is good among paving or on a patio where it can be trodden upon occasionally to release the scent. At midsummer the upright form provides upstanding pale mauve flower spikes, so leave this mint to flower and enjoy its alternative performance.

Mentha suaveolens, apple mint, is grown for its rounded hairy leaves with pretty edges and creamy white variegation. It is a most satisfactory plant at the edge of a terrace where the paving confines its activities and allows it the moist soil it needs. It is better in some shade despite the variegation, and is constantly sweet and fruity in aroma.

Mentha × villosa, and best in its form *alopecuroides*, is Bowles' mint or French mint. Tall-growing and vigorous with soft downy wrinkled leaves smelling deliciously clean of fresh sharp mint with fruity overtones, it is good in a border where its wanderings can be tolerated.

Origanum Three kinds of marjoram are commonly cultivated as herbs and all are excellent aromatic garden plants. Use them as border or path edging or grow them in raised beds and dry walls near the patio, or cultivate them in window boxes where the leaves can be rubbed occasionally to release their scent. Let them relax somewhere in full sunshine, and ensure good drainage especially in winter. Propagation is by seed, cuttings or division of established plants.

Origanum majorana, sweet or knotted marjoram, is usually cultivated as an annual and has brittle stems and soft grey, rather downy foliage. Dusky in general appearance, the plant produces pale lilac pink and white flowers in June and July held in little blob-like heads among the knotted clusters of leaves. Its fragrance is sweet and quite the best as a flavouring in cooking.

Origanum onites, pot marjoram, is somewhat rougher and more pungent in aroma but highly aromatic. It is a popular plant and the aroma persists to a certain extent even through the winter. Cut back the growth in spring to encourage fresh shoots. The flowers are pink or white, from June to August, and the leaves rounded; the whole plant forms good little hummocks. Marjoram is especially useful at the path edge where it can sprawl about.

Origanum vulgare, wild or common marjoram, sometimes confusingly called oregano, is easily recognised because it is altogether pinker in appearance than the other marjorams. The brittle stems are red and the flowers a lovely rose mauve, or sometimes white, and carried in rounded heads in June and July. They persist after their full flowering. A good golden-leaved form, 'Aureum' is particularly attractive in spring when the pretty rounded leaves can light up a pathway edge. As the summer progresses its leaves scorch badly so try to find a place where it is protected from the sun during the middle of the day without being in too much shade. A tiny form, 'Compactum', makes little sweet-smelling plants lovely for window boxes and containers generally, or for a trough of sweet-smelling plants. The leaves are a really bright golden green and the flowers open a little later in the summer than most marjorams.

A less attractive plant, though equally sweet-scented, is the golden-tipped marjoram which has white flowers and golden tips to most of the leaves, but by no means all of them. Regular cutting back will help to ensure new gold-painted leaves.

Perovskia atriplicifolia, **Russian sage,** is included although it is a semi-shrubby plant, because it adopts the habit of a herbaceous perennial and benefits from being cut right back each spring. Its silver white foliage and downy stems contrast strikingly with the soft blue flowers which are decked along the length of the stem in July and August. Bruise it to release a sage-like aroma. A handsome plant hailing from Afghanistan, it needs a sunny spot in well-drained soil. Cultivars 'Blue Haze' and 'Blue Spire' are both grown, the latter less attractive in foliage form. However, the added bonus of the frosted growth is a lovely attribute and it is very unusual to find a hairy plant that is aromatic.

Rosmarinus officinalis, **rosemary,** is known for its crisp evergreen spiky foliage that forms a good lax shrub. Gentle powder-blue flowers bloom officially in April and May but in many areas and in mild seasons from January onwards. The foliage is strongly aromatic and spicy, oily and distinctive, the shoots always turning upwards at the tips however sprawling the bush becomes. There is a fastigiate form catalogued as 'Miss Jessopp's Upright' with paler flowers. *R. officinalis prostratus* is in fact *R.* × *lavandulaceus,* which spreads mats of foliage speckled with flowers. This one is especially good at the top of a sunny bank or above a small retaining wall where it can be shown off to good effect and at the same time be given the sharp drainage it needs to see it through the winter.

Salvia This is an enormous genus, some of which have aromatic foliage to a greater or less extent and ranging from the blatantly bitter to fragrant. Garden sage, *Salvia officinalis,* is well known, varying in pungency according to the site. Perhaps in the scented garden its purple-leaved and tricolor variegated forms have a place; both are short-lived perennials with a woody base. For conservatory cultivation try *S. grahamii* for its aromatic leaves and scarlet flowers which will continue over a long period during the summer. Propagation of the sages is from seed where it sets, or by cuttings or layering. All of them love a sunny position, and need well drained fertile soil.

***Salvia rutilans* (S. *elegans*)** is a tender perennial of shrubby habit and is known as pineapple sage, because the fragrance of its leaves which surrenders to the merest brush is richly scented of pineapple. It is an interesting plant that will grow out of doors in very mild localities, and then merely for a season, and makes a good house plant or conservatory plant. It does not like full sunshine and needs to be watered regularly. It has beautifully soft-pointed foliage, every shoot suffused with damson purple. Propagate it by division or by summer cuttings.

***Salvia sclarea*, clary or muscatel sage,** is a biennial but is best cultivated as a half hardy annual, starting the seed as early as Christmas. It is finest in its form *turkestanica*. Variously coloured bracts, pink, mauve and blue adorn the flower spike and are particularly enchanting in the evening. A rich oily lemon scent with a distinct tang is perceptible when the plant is growing but as it matures the scent mellows and sweetens, earning it the name of muscatel sage.

Santolina Often overlooked, although popularly cultivated, the santolinas are among the best of sub-shrubs with interesting foliage. They all have bobble or button-like terminal yellow flowers in late summer and love really sun-baked well-drained spots. Use them as a border or driveway edging, or to cover a bank; most respond well to clipping so they can be kept within bounds. Propagation is from summer cuttings.

***Santolina chamaecyparissus*, cotton lavender,** forms a compact woody plant with silver thread-like foliage which is pungently aromatic when rubbed. The smaller form 'Nana' smells pleasanter.

***Santolina virens* (S. *rosmarinifolia rosmarinifolia*),** with emerald green foliage, is a short-lived perennial, disappearing quite quickly in many areas, but is successful when cultivated in a container. The heath-like foliage is very slightly oily to touch and therefore adheres to the skin. Its scent is very strongly camphorous and lingering.

Index

Page numbers in **bold** type refer to illustrations